THE HOLY SPIRIT

GUIDES TO THEOLOGY

Sponsored by the Christian Theological Research Fellowship

EDITORS

Sally Bruyneel • *Augsburg College*

Alan G. Padgett • *Luther Seminary*

David A. S. Fergusson • *University of Edinburgh*

Iain R. Torrance • *Princeton Theological Seminary*

Systematic theology is undergoing a renaissance. Conferences, journal articles, and books give witness to the growing vitality of the discipline. The Christian Theological Research Fellowship is one sign of this development. To stimulate further study and inquiry into Christian doctrine, we are sponsoring, with the William B. Eerdmans Publishing Company, a series of readable and brief introductions to theology.

This series of Guides to Theology is written primarily with students in mind. We also hope that pastors, church leaders, and theologians will find them to be useful introductions to the field. Our aim is to provide a brief introduction to the chosen field, followed by an annotated bibliography of important works, which should serve as an entrée to the topic. The books in this series will be of two kinds. Some volumes, like *The Trinity,* will cover standard theological *loci.* Other volumes will be devoted to various modern approaches to Christian theology as a whole, such as feminist theology or liberation theology. The authors and editors alike pray that these works will help further the faithful study of Christian theology in our time.

Visit our Web page at

http://www.ctrf.info

THE HOLY SPIRIT

F. LeRon Shults & Andrea Hollingsworth

WILLIAM B. EERDMANS PUBLISHING COMPANY
GRAND RAPIDS, MICHIGAN / CAMBRIDGE, U.K.

Published 2008 by
Wm. B. Eerdmans Publishing Co.
2140 Oak Industrial Drive N.E., Grand Rapids, Michigan 49505 /
P.O. Box 163, Cambridge CB3 9PU U.K.

Printed in the United States of America

13 12 11 10 09 08   7 6 5 4 3 2 1

Library of Congress Cataloging-in-Publication Data

Shults, F. LeRon.
The Holy Spirit / F. LeRon Shults & Andrea Hollingsworth.
p.   cm.   — (Guides to theology)
Includes bibliographical references and index.
ISBN 978-0-8028-2464-6 (pbk.: alk. paper)
1. Holy Spirit.   I. Hollingsworth, Andrea.   II. Title.

BT121.3.S58   2008
231'.3 — dc22

2008012009

www.eerdmans.com

To our spouses:

Elizabeth Shults

&

Ryan Hollingsworth

Contents

Acknowledgments   viii

Introduction   1

I: INTERPRETING THE TRANSFORMING EXPERIENCE OF THE HOLY SPIRIT   15

Patristic, Medieval, and Reformation Interpretations   17

Early and Late Modern Interpretations   57

II: ENGLISH-LANGUAGE RESOURCES ON THE HOLY SPIRIT   97

Annotated Bibliography   99

Index   151

Acknowledgments

This book emerged during a period of transition for both of us. We began to collaborate on the project in early 2006 while we were both still at Bethel Seminary in Minneapolis, Minnesota. In the fall of 2006 LeRon moved to Agder University in Norway, and Andrea began doctoral studies at Loyola University Chicago. We are grateful for the many friends and colleagues at these institutions who have encouraged us along the way. Four such people deserve special thanks. Alicia Gatto Petersen and Amos Yong provided helpful feedback on early drafts of various parts of the book. John Nelson and Ryan Hollingsworth carefully read through the penultimate draft and offered many constructive and critical comments. We are also thankful to Alan Padgett, who invited us to contribute to the Eerdmans series "Guides to Theology." It is always a pleasure working with Eerdmans Publishing Company; we offer special thanks to Jon Pott, Bill and Sam Eerdmans, Linda Bieze, Andrew Hoogheem, Jennifer Hoffman, Tonya Osterhouse, and Lara Sissell. Finally, we are grateful most of all to our supportive spouses, who provide the most significant interpersonal context within which we interpret our own transformative experience of the Spirit. This book is dedicated to them.

LeRon Shults
Andrea Hollingsworth
February 2008

Introduction

Christian theology is in the midst of an academic revival of interest in pneumatology — the study of the Spirit *(pneuma)* of God. Most treatments of the doctrine of the Holy Spirit in the middle of the twentieth century began with a complaint about the inadequacy of the Christian tradition's treatment of the "third person" of the Trinity (e.g., Hendry, 1956; Come, 1959). In the last few decades, however, reflection on the Spirit has come to the forefront of discussions within and across theological disciplines (e.g., systematic, biblical, and practical theology). Moreover, pneumatology has increasingly become a generative theme around which creative dialogue across religious traditions has flourished (e.g., ecumenism and interreligious dialogue).

In order to understand this dramatic growth of attention to the Holy Spirit in recent Christian theology, we must explore the factors that contributed to the waxing and waning of the tide of pneumatological interest throughout church history. Part I of this book identifies the key turning points and major thinkers who shaped the development of this doctrine, beginning with early Christian interpretations of the Spirit and concluding with a summary of contemporary trends in the ongoing task of reconstruction. For those who are interested in diving more deeply into particular aspects of the doctrine, this overview is supplemented by an annotated bibliography of English language resources in Part II.

This introduction provides an overview of the significance of our theme in the biblical witness and outlines some of the concerns that shape pneumatological discourse. This contribution to the Eerdmans Guides *to* Theology series is about the Guide *of* theological inquiry.

1

> When the Advocate [or Comforter] comes, whom I will send to you
> from the Father, the Spirit of truth who comes from the Father, he
> will testify on my behalf. . . . When the Spirit of truth comes, he will
> *guide* you into all the truth. (John 15:26; 16:13)

The promised Spirit is here depicted as a personal presence intimately related to the Father and the Son, a powerful presence that is both comforting and convincing, guiding believers into faithful fellowship with God.

Pneumatology is the attempt to interpret the transforming experience of this Spirit. As we will see, the Christian tradition has constantly struggled to make sense of this *holy* presence whose "otherness" confronts us and calls us toward transformation. Theological discourse about truth claims related to the Spirit of God must avoid two opposing dangers. On the one hand, we should be careful not to conclude all too quickly that we have already been led into all the truth. Taking a particular interpretation as the final and exhaustive truth is to deny the transcendent otherness of the Holy Spirit. On the other hand, acknowledging this inexhaustible otherness does not mean that we have no basis for discerning between interpretations. It is precisely within this tension, within this ongoing effort to know as we are known, that Christian theology attempts to bear witness to the transforming power of the personal presence of the Holy Spirit.

Our first step is to provide an initial description of the general contours of the biblical testimony to the experience of the Holy Spirit. We will return often to key scriptural images of the Spirit as we explore ways in which Christian theologians have interpreted these texts over the centuries, and so our introduction here will be relatively brief. Annotated bibliographies of comprehensive treatments of biblical scholarship on the relevant biblical texts on the Spirit are provided in Part II (cf. Montague, 1976, 2001; Heron, 1983; Congar, 1983; Fee, 1994; McIntyre, 1997; Dunn, 2006).

The Evocative Power of the Breath of Life

The authors of the Hebrew Bible used a variety of metaphors to describe their experience of the Spirit of God, including images of fluidity, fertility, and fire. Of all these ways of imagining the Spirit's relation to creation, it is the special connection to *life* that is picked up by the Nicene-Chalcedonian creed: "We believe in the Holy Spirit, the Lord, the Giver of Life." The power of the Holy Spirit is both the divine ground of the evocation of all life in general as well as the gracious presence that engenders particular experiences of transformed life (e.g., healing, prophecy).

The enlivening presence of the divine Spirit is depicted in both creation stories in Genesis, albeit in different ways. The emphasis in the first story is on the way in which the *ruach* (spirit, wind, breath) of God hovered over the watery chaos as creation was spoken (or called) into existence (Gen. 1:2). Here the differentiation of all forms of creaturely life is in view. In the second creation account, the concept of *ruach* is tied more specifically to the formation of human persons; having formed the first human from the dust, God "breathed into his nostrils the breath of life" (2:7). The abiding presence of this Spirit (breath) of God is a condition for ongoing human existence (6:3). The story of Noah makes clear that the ancient Hebrews acknowledged that animals too have the breath *(ruach)* of life from God (7:22). The Spirit is understood as especially connected to God's creative provision of the conditions for liveliness among all creatures.

The presence of the Spirit of God is not an explicit theme in the calling of Abraham, the arrival of Isaac, or the story of the conflict between Isaac's sons, Esau and Jacob; the concepts of blessing, facing, and naming play the major role in those narratives. Later in Genesis, however, the divine Spirit is understood as closely connected to revelation and empowerment. For example, Pharaoh responds to Joseph's spoken interpretation of his dream: "Can we find anyone else like this — one in whom is the spirit of God?" (41:38). Similarly the rescue of Moses and the deliverance of the people from the chariots of Pharaoh are interpreted as the effect of the very breath *(ruach)* of God: "At the blast of your nostrils the waters piled up . . . You blew with your wind, the sea covered them" (Ex. 15:8-10).

Later, Yahweh's guidance of the Israelites through the wilderness and into the Promised Land is explicitly understood as guidance by the Spirit who "fills" individuals for specific tasks (Ex. 31:3), or "comes upon" them in a way that empowers them for discernment or prophecy (Num. 11:25). In the book of Judges, those who gather up the community with new hope or deliver them from their enemies are interpreted as the ones upon whom the Spirit of the Lord has come. Also in Judges, prophetic leaders/warriors are made mighty by the Spirit of the Lord (3:10; 6:34; 11:29; 13:25). The experience of the Spirit's call to prophecy is ambiguous; it can be painful and does not automatically ensure holiness or guarantee just leadership. Some are led to prophesy day and night until they fall exhausted and naked, and others are driven out into the mountains and ravines (1 Sam. 19:19-24; cf. 2 Kings 2:16).

The wisdom literature also emphasizes that the divine *ruach* is the condition for human and indeed all creaturely life. "The spirit of God has made me, and the breath of the Almighty gives me life" (Job 33:4). This is not unique to humans, as the author of Ecclesiastes points out — humans and animals have the "same breath" (3:19-21). The poetry of the Psalms communicates a sense of the renewing presence of the Spirit which both establishes and sustains creaturely life in relation to God. Sometimes this presence is described as a general power that upholds, guides, forms, and gives life to *all* things: "When you send forth your spirit, they are created; and you renew the face of the ground" (Ps. 104:30). The presence of the divine *ruach* is universally present in and to creation. "Where can I go from your spirit? Or where can I flee from your presence" (Ps. 139:7). On the other hand, the life-giving *ruach* is also experienced as actively present in or among *specific* persons, renewing and redeeming them in special ways. For example, in David's prayer of contrition in Psalm 51:11 he entreats, "Do not cast me away from your presence, and do not take your holy spirit from me." This suggests that although the Spirit is understood as the general creative presence of God to creation, this power is beyond the control of human persons; transformation and indeed life itself are utterly dependent on the divine *ruach*.

In the prophetic literature, the Spirit also plays a unique role. The Spirit is depicted as a storm of judgment that sweeps everything away (Hos. 13:15), but also as a refreshing wind that turns the wilderness into an orchard (Isa. 32:15-18). In the exilic and postexilic writings, prophecy is seen as a direct work of the revealing Spirit of Yahweh (Ezek. 2:2; 3:24) which disturbs as it convicts of infidelity and injustice, warns of impending judgment (Zech. 7:12; Neh. 9:30), purges the people "with the spirit of judgment and with the spirit of fire" (Isa. 4:4), and consumes the sinners in Zion (Isa. 33:11). But the Spirit also comforts as it drenches the LORD's people with blessing and hope for renewed life: "I will pour water on the thirsty land, and streams on the dry ground; I will pour my spirit upon your descendents, and my blessing on your offspring" (Isa. 44:3). Thus through the prophets, Yahweh's Spirit (disturbingly) judges, warns, and calls to repentance as well as (comfortingly) promises future redemption.

One also finds a fascinating connection between the divine Spirit and the transformation of the human voice in the prophetic literature. The Spirit comes upon Isaiah and fills his mouth with everlasting words (Isa.

59:21). Ezekiel is commanded by the LORD's Spirit to speak to the valley of dry bones; as he does so, the divine Spirit goes forth through his breath, voice, and lips, and the dry bones are brought to life — a symbol of Israel's future hope and renewal (Ezek. 37:1-10). Micah senses that the Spirit of the LORD is filling him with power to loudly declare to Israel her sin (Mic. 3:8). Joel, speaking in the first person for God, announces a day of coming redemption when the Spirit will be poured out on all flesh: "Your sons and your daughters shall prophesy, your old men shall dream dreams, and your young men shall see visions. Even on the male and female slaves, in those days, I will pour out my spirit" (Joel 2:28-29). These and other passages suggest that Israel's prophets understood themselves as powerful mouthpieces of the disturbing and comforting divine voice.

During the exile, the Hebrew interpretation of the *ruach* of Yahweh was shaped by encounter with the religious philosophy of their Babylonian captors. One can hear echoes of the dualistic cosmology of Zoroastrianism in the Dead Sea Scrolls, which make extensive use of the opposition between the "spirit of truth" and "the spirit of falsehood" (cf. Heron, 1983; Breck, 1991). The apocryphal literature makes occasional use of the phrase "Holy Spirit" (e.g., Sus. 1:45; 2 Esdr. 14:22), a term used only twice in the Hebrew Bible, in Psalm 51:11 and Isaiah 63:10-11. In Hellenistic Judaism during this period (the "Diaspora") the idea of divine *Sophia* — or Wisdom personified in female form — is connected to the idea of *ruach*. "For wisdom is more mobile than any motion; because of her pureness she pervades and penetrates all things. For she is a breath *(ruach)* of the power of God . . ." (Wis. 7:24-27). Her presence is both universal and particular — she renews all things, but also "passes into holy souls" making them "friends of God and prophets" (7:27).

Sophia/Wisdom had already been personified in Proverbs as the LORD's cocreator who rejoices in the inhabited world and the human race (Prov. 8:31). She calls out to human beings, her children, admonishing them to listen to her voice: "Hear instruction and be wise, and do not neglect it" (8:33). Above we observed that Spirit and voice are closely related in the prophetic literature, and here too it is notable that *Sophia*/Wisdom is "calling" her children into a future in which they share in intimate knowledge of one another and God. Her voice invites humanity to maturity, life, and insight (9:6).

The interpretation of the experience of the life-giving Spirit is characterized both by continuity and discontinuity through the various genre of the Hebrew Bible. The interpretation of what happened to Jesus, and to his followers, draws deeply upon the Jewish tradition in which he and they were immersed, but the radical disclosure of the unimaginable power of the evocative breath of life in the resurrection of Christ opens up a whole new hermeneutical and existential horizon for understanding and experiencing the Holy Spirit.

The Spirit of the One who Raised Jesus from the Dead

The Hebrew idea of the Spirit of God as a creative and renewing presence was taken up by many of the authors of the New Testament, but they interpreted their experience of transformation in light of the resurrection of Jesus of Nazareth by the One whom he called Father. This is the basis for what would later come to be called the doctrine of the Trinity. As we will see throughout Part I, Christian pneumatology is, whether implicitly or explicitly, always spelled out within the context of trinitarian discourse, and always plays a constitutive and regulative role within that discourse. The important point at this introductory stage is recognizing the ways in which the relation of Jesus Christ to the Spirit opened up new ways of understanding how God calls human beings into holiness, freedom, and new life.

An emphasis on the enlivening and renewing presence of the Spirit pervades the Pauline literature. "The Spirit of him who raised Jesus from the dead dwells in you . . . [he] will give life to your mortal bodies also through his Spirit that dwells in you" (Rom. 8:11). The "you" in this text is plural, and Paul goes out of his way to connect the experience of the Holy Spirit to the flourishing of the community throughout his letter to the Romans. God's love "has been poured into our hearts through the Holy Spirit" (5:5). The "Spirit of life in Christ Jesus . . . [sets] free from the law of sin and death" (8:2). The present experience of the transforming Spirit makes us "groan inwardly" as we yearn for "the redemption of our bodies" (8:23). The Spirit is the source of the community's love, freedom, and hope for renewal.

One of Paul's central themes is the way in which the Holy Spirit creates, upholds, and enlivens the community of believers. The "gifts" of the Spirit, which are manifested through individual voices, are primarily intended for communal contexts and for the common good of everyone (1 Cor. 12). Christians should not grieve the Spirit by using their voices in ways that tear each other down (cf. Eph. 4:29-32), nor should they quench the Spirit by despising the utterances of prophets (1 Thess. 5:19-20). The Spirit gives life (2 Cor. 3:6) and freedom (2 Cor. 3:17) to the people of God, calling them toward ever-intensifying transformation together: "And all of us, with unveiled faces, seeing the glory of the Lord as though reflected in a mirror, are being transformed into the same image from one degree of glory to another; for this comes from the Lord, the Spirit" (2 Cor. 3:18).

It is clear from these and other contexts that Paul does not understand the Spirit simply as an abstract power, but as a personal presence intimately connected to God's redemptive work in Christ. Paul often attributes the hope of the community to the comforting and assuring presence of the Spirit who is a "seal," a "first installment," and a "guarantee" of future resurrection glory for all those who are in Christ (2 Cor. 1:21-22; 2 Cor. 5:5). Paul's letters also point to ways in which the transforming experience of the Spirit can feel disturbing and disorienting, as well as comforting and reorienting in the concrete life of the community. Those who are led by the Spirit are not subject to law, but Spirit-filled living results in loving, patient, gentle attitudes and actions toward others (Gal. 5:18-23).

Each of the Gospels emphasizes the significance of the way in which the Spirit of God is related to Jesus of Nazareth. Mark and Matthew both begin with descriptions of John the Baptist proclaiming a baptism of repentance and pointing to the arrival of one who would baptize with the Holy Spirit (Mark 1:8; Matt. 3:11). In Jesus' baptism by John in the Jordan, he hears the voice of his Father declaring him his "beloved Son," and receives the promised anointing of the Spirit, which descends on him like a dove (Mark 1:9-11; Matt. 3:13-17; cf. Isa. 11:1-4). This event inaugurates his ministry as the Christ — the long-anticipated, Spirit-anointed Messiah who would preach the good news and deliver the people from bondage (Mark 3:23-30; Matt. 12:28; cf. Isa. 61:1-2). This suggests that it was the presence of the Holy Spirit in Jesus' life that made him particularly interesting for the earliest chroniclers of the gospel.

The author of the Gospel of Luke and the Book of Acts places even more attention on the Spirit than did Mark and Matthew. Like in the Hebrew Bible, where the evocative Spirit hovered over creation and enlivened the voices of the prophets of Yahweh, in Luke-Acts there is an emphasis on the ways that the Spirit anoints or rests upon bodies and voices, transforming them into mediators of the divine presence. In Luke, the Holy Spirit fills John the Baptist from before the time of his birth (1:15). John is portrayed as the Spirit-filled voice in the wilderness who echoes the cry of the prophet Isaiah — "prepare the way of the Lord, make his paths straight" (3:4; cf. Isa. 40:3). The Spirit is described as hovering over Mary's pregnancy (1:35); resting upon Simeon the priest, who then envelops the child Jesus in his arms and prophesies over him (2:25-35); and descending upon Jesus at his baptism in the presence of the Father (3:22). The Holy Spirit not only anoints bodies and enlivens voices, but also calls them outward toward serving others, into the world to do the work of the divine kingdom of peace and justice. The Spirit summons Jesus out into the wilderness (4:1), fills him with power for ministry (4:14), and anoints him to preach and proclaim freedom from oppression (4:18-19).

The Book of Acts tells the story of the Spirit's calling and empowering of the early followers of Christ. The Holy Spirit falls on the bodies of the disciples in tongues of fire at Pentecost, filling them with power to voice loudly and clearly the good news of the risen Christ to all people (2:1-13). Furthermore, the Spirit is poured out on the Gentiles during the early Christian missions (10:44). This takes place because the Father has given the Holy Spirit to the Son, the Son poured it out to the disciples (2:33), and now the disciples — having seen and heard the truth of the gospel — are compelled and empowered by God's Spirit to spread the good news "in Jerusalem, in all Judea and Samaria, and to the ends of the earth" (1:8). Peter, however, is tempted to resist the Spirit who calls him toward radical love of outsiders. He has to learn that God's Spirit is summoning him out of Jerusalem — his comfort zone — and into fellowship with Cornelius and other "unclean" Gentiles (10:28). While this is initially disturbing to Peter who has tried to claim the center by excluding others from fellowship, it is comforting to those who now find themselves enfolded into the community of the people of God in the fellowship of the Spirit.

The Johannine literature offers a new and distinctive emphasis on the Spirit. The Gospel of John, one of the last books in the canon to be written, offers us an interpretation of the experience of the Spirit that has the benefit of several decades of reflection on the way in which the Spirit transforms the community. It also provides intimations of what will later become the doctrine of the Trinity. In John, the Father gives the Spirit to the Son (1:32), the Son sends the Spirit (16:7; 20:22), and the Spirit glorifies the Son by taking what is the Son's and the Father's, and declaring it to the world (16:14-15).

The voice of the Spirit is portrayed as both soothing and disquieting. Jesus reminds Nicodemus that the Spirit is, like the wind, uncontrollable and unpredictable (3:8-9). The Spirit is the Advocate, or Comforter, who will teach and console the disciples after Jesus departs (14:16, 26; 16:6-8). Later John also makes it clear that the Spirit also convicts the world of sin (16:8). The promised "Spirit of truth" is a comfortingly vocal presence who testifies on Jesus' behalf (15:26) and guides the disciples into truth by speaking "whatever he hears," and "declaring . . . the things that are to come" (16:13-15). In an intimate and reassuring gesture Jesus breathes on the disciples and says, "receive the Holy Spirit," which empowers them to forgive (20:22-23). This metaphor is perhaps linked with the Hebrew concept of *ruach* — the evocative, creative, and renewing breath of life.

As we will see throughout the historical narrative of Part I, and illustrate throughout the bibliographic resources in Part II, Christian pneumatology has always tried to remain rooted in this biblical tradition. However, every attempt to interpret the experience of this transforming presence has been shaped by the contexts in which it is embedded. Understanding the factors that have shaped the Christian story of struggling to live in and testify to the Spirit can help us understand our own place in this story and facilitate our own attempts to articulate the good news about the Spirit of the One who raised Christ from the dead and now dwells in us.

Interpretation and Transformation

Our basic approach in this book will be to trace the key issues, persons, and debates in pneumatology, beginning with the earliest Christian communities and ending with several recent reconstructive theological proposals. However, the study of the Spirit is much too dynamic to be reduced to a chronicle of names and dates. Our strategy, therefore, will be to use the relation between interpretation and transformation as a leitmotif throughout our discussion.

It is important to emphasize that pneumatological interpretation always occurs in the context of dealing with experiences of *transformation*. By underlining this throughout the book we hope to demonstrate (and contribute to) one of the most dominant trends in contemporary discussions of the doctrine: the linking of Spirit to spirituality. If we take the latter in a general sense as indicating the ways in which we interpret and attend to the transformation of our relation to God, to our neighbors, and to our selves, then it makes sense to ask how the Holy Spirit is related to these concerns of the human spirit. This is not a book about spiritual formation or the renewal of the church, but inevitably these issues come to bear on our discussion of the Spirit. The need for this integrative approach will become particularly evident as we explore some of the other key trends in pneumatology, in dialogue with movements such as feminist theology, liberation theology, and ecumenism; and as we explore the astonishing expansion of Pentecostalism worldwide.

The connection between Spirit and spirituality seems increasingly obvious in late modernity, but this has not always been so. Since the seventeenth century, pneumatology proper has registered hardly any effect on the literature of spirituality. Conversely, many systematic theological treatments of the doctrine of the Holy Spirit have been relatively detached from the concrete concerns of practical Christian life. The healing of this dichotomy has been facilitated by a broader and growing interest in integrating spirituality and theology in general (cf. McIntosh, 1998; Sheldrake, 1998; Chan, 1998; Humphrey, 2006; Shults & Sandage, 2006). In this introductory book we hope to contribute to this development in pneumatology by paying as much attention to the mystics as to the scholastics and by focusing on the practical as well as the theoretical factors that shape our understanding of the Holy Spirit. Theologically attending to (spiritual) transformation leads us to reflect on the ways we understand and articulate our experience of the disturbing and comforting presence of the Spirit of God.

In the context of an academic guide to theology, it is not enough simply to point out that our theme is the interpretation of transformation; we must also emphasize the dynamics involved in the transformation of *interpretation*. We have already seen how the interpretation of the Spirit was shaped by the various contexts within which the Hebrew Bible and New Testament books were written. And throughout Part I we will discover that the debates over formulations in the doctrine of the Holy Spirit continue to bear the marks of the cultural and political contexts in which they occurred.

For this reason we will try to point out some of the basic philosophical categories that have shaped (and continue to shape) pneumatological discourse. To a greater or lesser extent, theologians engage and appropriate the linguistic categories of the cultural contexts in which they operate. This does not mean that doctrinal formulations are wholly determined by such categories, for the transforming experience of the Spirit cannot be captured or constrained by human concepts or practices. However, it does mean that understanding *why* the interpretation of the Spirit has shifted will require paying attention to the shifts in the use and meaning of the very concepts of "holy" and "Spirit" over time. While such a claim may have been controversial during the early modern period, it almost goes without saying in late modernity that all theology is shaped by the philosophical categories that structure the contours of any particular cultural discourse.

But it does not quite go without saying. Many new students of theology are initially resistant to the idea that all experience (even religious experience of the Spirit) is interpreted. An exposition of the impact of developments in the philosophy of science on Christian theology is beyond the task of this book, but several recent treatments of the relation between philosophy and theology are available for interested readers.[1] Our more limited goal is simply to illustrate the mutuality of interpretation and transformation throughout the historical development of the doctrine. In this introductory volume, we are forced to risk oversimplification. But if the following overview sheds some light on the complex developments in pneumatology over the last two millennia it will have been worth the risk.

In Part I we will sometimes refer to three ancient and competing "schools" of philosophy that have been particularly influential on Christian theology: Platonism, Aristotelianism, and Stoicism. It is important to recognize that the philosophical world into which the Christian religion was born was shaped significantly by what has come to be called Middle Platonism, an eclectic philosophical approach which flourished from around 130 B.C. to 200 A.D. Following Plato for the most part, it also adopted and adapted aspects of Aristotelianism as well as elements of the materialistic and atomistic cosmology of many of the Stoics. The New Testament writings emerged in this context, and over the last century biblical scholarship has increasingly attended to the way in which, for example, the letters of Paul have Stoicism as one of their main dialogue partners (cf. Engberg-Pedersen, 2000).

Platonic and neo-Platonic philosophy took the upper hand during the first few centuries in which Christian theology unfolded. During the Mid-

---

1. For resources on the relationships between philosophy and theology, we recommend Diogenes Allen, *Philosophy for Understanding Theology* (Atlanta: John Knox Press, 1985); John Caputo, *Philosophy and Theology* (Nashville: Abingdon, 2006); Kelly James Clark, Richard Lints, and James K. A. Smith, *101 Key Terms in Philosophy and Their Importance for Theology* (Louisville: Westminster John Knox, 2004); Ingolf Dalferth, *Philosophy and Theology* (Eugene, Ore.: Wipf & Stock, 2001); and F. LeRon Shults, *The Postfoundationalist Task of Theology* (Grand Rapids: Eerdmans, 1999).

dle Ages, Aristotle's philosophy was rediscovered in the West and, through Thomas Aquinas among others, it registered a deep influence on Roman Catholic theology in particular. During the Renaissance, interest in Stoicism and other ancient sources was renewed, and this shaped both the Protestant Reformation and the rise of modern science. Because each of these vying "schools" of philosophy affected the understanding of human transformation in relation to the divine, they of course had a considerable influence on Christian pneumatology.

It is also important to realize that both Platonism and Aristotelianism tended to privilege the concept of *logos* (rational order) over the concept of *pneuma* (dynamic movement), which partly explains why christology (the enfleshment of the divine *Logos*) received more attention during this period than pneumatology (the indwelling of the divine *Spirit*). This privileging was less explicit in the third strand of Middle Platonism, but even the Stoics sometimes seemed to conflate *pneuma* and *logos,* a habit taken over by some early Christian theologians, as we shall see. Interpretations of the Holy Spirit throughout history have certainly not been *controlled* by philosophical approaches, but they have no doubt been *conditioned* by critical engagement with them. Understanding how this worked in the past can help us today as we reflect on how to interpret our own experience of transformation.

So how did these philosophical developments impact pneumatology? A full response to this question is beyond the scope of an introductory textbook, but we can point to three categories that are particularly relevant for the doctrine of the Spirit. These are matter, person, and force:

- How can we imagine the divine Spirit in relation to the "material" world of creation?
- How is the "personal" presence of the Holy Spirit to be understood in relation to the personhood of the Father and the Son?
- How is the infinitely powerful "force" of the Spirit of God related to the finitude of human freedom?

The answers to these pneumatological questions are partially dependent on the way in which one defines the concepts embedded within them. With that in mind, let us explore briefly how each of the classical philosophical schools approaches these issues, and the implications this might have for the doctrine of the Holy Spirit.

In the history of Western philosophy, "matter" has often been conceptualized in dialectical opposition to the concept of "spirit" (or some other term for the *im*-material, whether form, soul, energy, life, mind, or thought). Plato is perhaps most well known for his distinction between the realm of the Forms (or Ideas) and the realm of matter. The changing material world is subject to alteration and decay, while the ideal (immaterial or intelligible) world is unchanging and eternal. Aristotle, on the other hand, rejected the notion of two realms and argued that matter and form are constitutively intertwined within every particular thing. Many of the Stoics argued that all things are composed of atomic (un-cuttable), material parts. This does not mean that they did not believe in God or in spirit, but that they viewed *pneuma* (divine and human) as matter, albeit very finely diffused matter. For the most part, Platonism and Aristotelianism dominated the philosophical and theological landscape up until the rise of modern science, which increasingly relied on Stoic materialism, atomism, and determinism (see below). On the question of the nature of matter, Christian pneumatology has been more deeply influenced by Plato and Aristotle than by the Stoics, as we shall see. While this has helped to clarify the transcendence of the Holy Spirit from the material world, it has sometimes led to a denigration of the latter, and made it difficult to make sense of the real, pervading, enlivening presence of the Spirit to and in the cosmos.

The way in which one defines "person" is also important for pneumatology, especially as this bears on one's understanding of the relation of the Spirit to the other two trinitarian persons. Plato and Aristotle were both critical of the popular Greek anthropomorphic understanding of the gods, in which divine beings were susceptible to human passions like fear, anger, jealousy, and so forth. Instead, these philosophers argued for an understanding of God as beyond such categories, either as the immutable Form of the Good (Plato) or the Unmoved Mover (Aristotle). However, their conceptions of *human* personhood, which focused on the relation of the substance of the body to the substance of the soul in the individual, had an often unnoticed impact on the doctrine of the Trinity. The stress on the individual soul and its faculties of intellect and volition, which was even more dominant among the Stoics, is evident in the sixth-century philosopher Boethius's influential definition of person as "an individual substance of a rational nature." If this is what it means to be a person, how can we speak of the Spirit, the Father, and the Son as all persons without collapsing into tri-theism? As we will see, one of the most popular ways of spelling out the doctrine of the Trinity depicted the Holy Spirit as the will (and the Son as the intellect) of God. Notice that Boethius' definition emphasizes intellect over will. This philosophical predilection contributed to the rise and complicated the discussion of the notion of the Spirit's procession from the Father and the Son *(filioque)*.

In Christian life the Holy Spirit is experienced as a real and transforming "force," but the way in which this category is defined also ramifies into theological formulations of this doctrine. The Spirit is a power that moves the people of God, but how are we to interpret this experience in relation to other forces in the world, including our own power to respond? For Plato all movement in the world is the result of active spiritual principles that enliven material things so they participate in the Forms. The divine creative principle, which he called the Demiurge, created the World-Soul, which is diffused throughout the "body" of the universe. Aristotle's theory of force was more developed and emerged out of his analysis of the movement of particular things. In addition to material and formal causes (see above) Aristotle argued that every change also requires an "efficient" and a "final" cause, that is, an agent who moves it and a goal toward which it moves. As the Unmoved Mover, God is the ultimate final cause in relation to whose perfection all things are oriented. We will see how Platonic and Aristotelian conceptions of force or movement shaped various theological proposals in the doctrine of the Holy Spirit, especially up through the early modern period. For some Stoics, everything is determined by the movement of atoms. They spoke of the divine *pneuma* as the creative fire that holds all things in tension, and said human souls have a spark of the divine within them. However, human motion (like all motion) is determined by their dispositional relation to the pneumatic fire of the cosmos. With the rise of modern science, this more fatalistic conception of force registered an effect on much Christian theology, including the understanding of the powerful presence of the divine Spirit in the work of human transformation.

This brief introduction has only touched upon the many important biblical themes, philosophical issues, and practical concerns that have shaped pneumatological discourse. We will often return to these and others as we move through a short overview of the doctrine of the Holy Spirit in Part I. Resources for more detailed study are provided in Part II. However deeply you desire to immerse yourself in this ongoing theological dialogue, we hope that this guide will quicken in you a desire to be immersed in the Guide to all truth.

I. INTERPRETING THE TRANSFORMING EXPERIENCE OF THE HOLY SPIRIT

Patristic, Medieval,
and Reformation Interpretations

The complex tapestry of pneumatology has been woven over the centuries by women and men who have experienced the transforming presence of the Spirit. The threads they have used have been drawn primarily from Scripture, but the themes and patterns they have made have also been conditioned by the cultural context of the church over the centuries. Pneumatological confession is a chorus, to switch metaphors, of diverse voices that are sometimes harmonic, sometimes cacophonic; sometimes jubilant, sometimes restrained. As we listen to this choir of voices we are invited to join in. Our task in this chapter and the next is to try to understand the legacy that has been left to us by a variety of Christian theologians — scholastics, mystics, cynics, and enthusiasts — so that we can carry on that legacy in our own contexts.

Early Christian Interpretations of the Spirit

It is important to remember that during the first few centuries of the Christian church, before the formation of the biblical canon and before the age of the ecumenical councils, debates over questions about the nature and work of the Holy Spirit were complicated by the lack of any clear authoritative consensus on the criteria by which to answer such questions. Some of the early "apostolic" fathers — so called because they were alleged to have been in direct contact with some of the original twelve apostles — claimed that their own writings were as authoritative as those of the apostles since it was the same Spirit who inspired them. For the most part, the treatment of the Holy Spirit among these theologians (such as Clement of Rome, Ignatius of Antioch, and Polycarp of Smyrna) dealt with the Spirit's role in biblical inspiration, in the provision of charismatic gifts (especially prophecy), and in guiding moral life.

The debates over the relation of the Spirit to the Father and the Son would emerge only later, in the context of the great councils, but the groundwork for these discussions was already being laid in the second century. As the Christian religion began to stabilize after the success of early missionary work, its intellectual leaders were increasingly able to engage the philosophical milieu of their era in order to explain their faith. The popular new religion attracted the critical attention of many philosophers who challenged its credibility. The early "apologists" were those who offered a defense *(apologia)* of the intelligibility of faith in Christ, seeking to defend Christianity against all kinds of accusations, including atheism, cannibalism, incest, superstition, and treason.

The Middle Platonic emphasis on *logos* over *pneuma* created a philosophical context in which these theologians quite naturally turned most of their energy toward defending faith in Christ as the *Logos* of God. This is evident, for example, in the mid second-century *Shepherd of Hermas* (1994), whose unknown author did not distinguish between the divine *Logos* and the *Pneuma*, equating the Holy Spirit with the Son of God. In the *Shepherd* and other works of this time, the Spirit is usually depicted as playing a sanctifying role in the context of the moral battle between good and evil forces within individual believers. At this early stage theologians were not primarily concerned with clarifying or defending the deity of the Spirit in relation to the Father and the Son.

One can also see this in the writings of the most influential early apologist, Justin Martyr (100-165 A.D.), whose focus on the *Logos* sometimes seems to downplay any real differentiation between the Word and the Spirit. For example, even in discussing prophecy (traditionally linked to the Spirit) in his *First Apology,* Justin attributes the power of the inspiring Spirit to the *Logos.* When he discusses the virgin conception of Christ in light of Isaiah's prophecy, he argues that it is wrong "to understand the Spirit and the power of God as anything else than the Word, who is the first-born of God. . . . the prophets are inspired by no other than the Divine Word" (XXXIII; 1994, p. 174).[1] Such

---

1. Most scholars refer to the works of patristic and medieval authors by indicating the book in Roman numerals and the subsections of that book in Arabic numerals. When citing

a conflation of pneumatology into christology seems to render the former superfluous.

This way of correlating Word and Spirit in Justin appears to be in tension, however, with his earlier claim that the Son is held in the "second place" in relation to the one true God, and the Spirit in the "third place" (XIII; 1994, p. 167). Some scholars see this latter subordination of the Spirit to the Son as an example of the application of the Platonic notion of "emanation" to the Christian idea of the relation of God to the world. On this neo-Platonic view, the *Logos,* or intellectual principle, emanates from the unchanging One, and the Spirit, or World-Soul, emanates from the *Logos;* but eventually all things return to the One. This popular philosophical "trinity" was condemned by later church councils, but it was often utilized in these early debates. During the second century, most of the focus of theology was on how this new religion understood and facilitated salvation, so one could argue that Justin was only making a point about the way in which the Word and the Spirit work together in the redemption of the world. At any rate, his choice of this language illustrates the influence of Middle Platonism on the emergence of Christian pneumatological discourse.

One of the most significant challenges facing the early Christian church was the popularity of Gnosticism, which took the Platonic metaphysical dualism between the realm of the intelligible and the realm of the material and turned it into a soteriological dualism, in which the mind *(nous)* could and should escape from the body. The Gnostics taught that matter is intrinsically evil, and so flesh cannot participate in salvation. This was not only problematic for the Christian belief in the Incarnation (that is, that the Word was made flesh; John 1:14), but also for the Christian experience of the healing of the body and the bodily manifestations of the Spirit in community. Most Gnostics claimed that salvation required a special *gnosis* (knowledge), which is available only to a select few.

Many Christians were tempted by Gnosticism's emphasis on the spiritual life and its enthusiastic embrace of the ecstatic experiences of illumination. However, it was difficult to square Gnostic spirituality with the

---

these authors, we have provided these references first in order to facilitate finding them for readers who may not have access to the latest scholarly editions. Following the semicolon in each case is an author/year reference to a work listed in Part II of this book, typically a relatively accessible contemporary translation of the text.

biblical valuation of (material) creation, which promises that the Spirit will be poured out on all flesh and emphasizes a bodily resurrection. Worrisome, too, was the elitism practiced by the Gnostics. Many early Christians, however, did accept the metaphysical dualism of Gnosticism. The strong distinction between spirit and matter, which was equated with that between good and evil, led Marcion, a wealthy and popular late second-century Christian leader, to argue that there must be a radical difference between the God of the Old Testament — who created matter — and the God of love and light revealed in the New Testament. Marcionism was condemned for a variety of reasons, but for our purposes it is interesting to note that Marcion, like many of the apostolic fathers and apologists, did not develop a clear articulation of the nature of the Holy Spirit, who was often simply identified with Christ (or the *Logos*).

Gnosticism was also one of the main targets of Irenaeus of Lyons (130-202 A.D.), often considered the most influential of the early church fathers. He used the metaphor of the "two hands of God" to express the way in which the Son and the Spirit are operative in creation and redemption, including the transformation of real fleshly existence. In Book V of *Against Heresies*, he begins by emphasizing that Jesus himself had a real body, that what was generated by the Holy Spirit in Mary was a "holy thing," and that at his baptism the Spirit descended upon real "flesh and blood" (V.1.2-3; 1994, p. 527). The same applies to the Spirit's transformation of believers, whose bodies are called temples of the Spirit and are promised bodily resurrection by the power of the Spirit. Irenaeus clearly has the dualism of the Gnostics in mind when he asks, "How then is it not the utmost blasphemy to allege, that the temple of God [the human body], in which the Spirit of the Father dwells, and the members of Christ, do not partake of salvation, but are reduced to perdition?" (V.6.2; 1994, p. 532). Irenaeus also emphasizes the role of the Spirit in the constitution of the church, forging a link between pneumatology and ecclesiology: "For where the Church is, there is the Spirit of God; and where the Spirit of God is, there is the Church" (III.23.1; 1994, p. 458).

Questions about the person and work of the Holy Spirit came to the forefront of discussion with the development of the Montanist movement in the second century. The leader of this "New Prophecy," as it came to be known, was a man named Montanus who, along with two women, Priscilla and Maximilla, claimed to be a direct mouthpiece of the Holy Spirit. The end of the world was one of the dominant themes in their ecstatic utterances. In his *Church History,* fourth-century theologian and historian Eusebius gives a scathing appraisal of the New Prophecy. According to him, the movement's followers had claimed that Montanus was the Paraclete — the Spirit of truth promised in John 14. Eusebius cites an anonymous critic who attributes the ecstasies not to the Holy Spirit but to the devil, who had "secretly excited and inflamed their understandings. . . . And filled them [Montanus, Priscilla, and Maximilla] with the false spirit, so that they talked wildly and unreasonably and strangely" (V.16; 1994, pp. 229, 231).

It was not simply the animated and expressive character of their prophecies that led many theologians to resist the movement. What its opponents found more worrisome was the Montanist claim that not only had the Spirit's revelation not ceased with the apostolic era, but that it now continued exclusively through their utterances. Montanism was condemned and ultimately exterminated under the reign of Constantine, a process that occurred over time as greater emphasis was placed on the church hierarchy and the authority of bishops, and less on the presence of the gifts *(charismata)* of the Spirit, as the basis for identifying the church. Some contemporary theologians have argued that Montanism has been unfairly judged throughout church history, and that some aspects of the movement might be retrieved as a legitimate source for understanding charismatic and Pentecostal renewal today (cf. Burgess, 1984; Tabbernee, 2001).

Tertullian (b. 150 A.D.), who has been called "the Church's first important pentecostal theologian" (Burgess, 1984, p. 63), was pro-Montanist and defended the spirituality of the New Prophecy. His pneumatology, which is spread out through several major treatises, is deeply connected to his Montanist experience of the Spirit. In his *Treatise on the Soul* he states that it is only by ecstasy, "in which the sensuous soul stands out of itself, in a way which even resembles madness," that true prophecy can be expressed (XLV; 1994, p. 223). However, this does not mean that "anything goes" in the name of ecstasy. In *On Modesty,* Tertullian refers to the Holy Spirit as the "Determiner of discipline itself" (XI; 1994, p. 85), and throughout his works he emphasizes that true spirituality is characterized by an ascetic lifestyle, which requires discipline and abstinence from worldly pleasures.

Tertullian plays a particularly important role in the development of the terminology that later came to dominate debates over the doctrine of the Trinity. He was the first to apply the Latin word *trinitas* to God, and the first to use the term *persona* to describe Father, Son, and Spirit. In his treatise *Against Praxeas*, he reflects in a sustained and systematic way upon Father, Son, and Holy Spirit (I–XXXI; 1994, pp. 597-627). The persons are "three . . . not in condition, but in degree; not in substance, but in form; not in power, but in aspect; yet of one substance, and of one condition, and of one power" (II; 1994, p. 598). He describes the emanation of the Spirit from the Father through the Son, "as the stream out of the river is third from the fountain, or as the apex of the ray is third from the sun" (VIII; 1994, p. 603). Several chapters later he articulates how the Paraclete's personal existence is distinct: "Thus the connection of the Father in the Son, and of the Son in the Paraclete, produces three coherent Persons, who are yet distinct One from Another. These Three are one essence, not one Person, as it is said, 'I and my Father are One,' in respect of unity of substance, not singularity of number" (XXI; 1994, p. 621). Tertullian's efforts to explicate the relations among the persons of the Trinity provided language and set the stage for many later attempts at clarifying the doctrine of the Holy Spirit.

Another aspect of Middle Platonism that impacted some Christian formulations of the relations among the trinitarian persons was the belief that there are three basic principles for explaining the origin and order of the cosmos: God, Ideas, and Matter. On this philosophical model, God is beyond the universe and has no direct relation to it. The Ideas (or Forms) were understood as existing in (or as) the divine *Nous* (Mind). Building on Plato's notion of the Demiurge, or creative spirit, many Middle Platonists thought of the *Logos* as a mediating principle through which the material cosmos was given order and form. Theologians like Clement of Alexandria (150-215 A.D.) appropriated this language to articulate the relation of the Father to the Son. The danger with this approach, from a Christian point of view, was that it could easily be taken (and was in fact later taken) to imply that the Son (as *Logos*) was not divine in the same way as God the "Father of all." The philosophical "trinity" of this form of Middle Platonism, in which the role of the World-Soul was less significant, made it even less compatible with the biblical understanding of the relation of the Holy Spirit to Christ and to the One he called Father. Those who interpreted their experience of transformation with such categories often philosophically subordinated the passionate liveliness of the Spirit to the rational ordering of the *Logos*, or subsumed the former into the latter.

For Origen (b. 185 A.D.), one of the most controversial theologians of the early church, the Spirit is explicitly equated with Mind. In *On First Priniciples* he argues that the Holy Spirit is an "intellectual existence" (I.1.3; 1994, p. 243). To say "God is Spirit," he argues, is to say that God is a simple "intellectual nature," and "the Mind" from which all other minds take their beginning. In addition to this Middle Platonist tendency to privilege rationality, Origen sometimes seems to share the Gnostic aversion to embodiment and materiality. God is incorporeal, "without any material substance, and without partaking in any degree of a bodily adjunct" (I.6.4; 1994, p. 262). It is true that this clarifies the relation between God (the Father) and the *Logos* (Mind) in distinction from the corporeal world, but many later theologians would find such a formulation problematic for making sense of the doctrine of the Incarnation.

Origen's philosophical preferences registered an effect not only on his doctrine of God (as Spirit), but also on his understanding and practice of spirituality. Like most other Christian theologians before him, Origen consistently linked the Holy Spirit with human moral and spiritual transformation. His struggle to escape embodied desire led him to practice rather severe forms of ascetic discipline; he is alleged to have removed parts of his body that he experienced as a source of temptation. For Origen, the Holy Spirit only indwells the minds of the pure, or those who are being made pure through unceasing sanctification. He believed that the Spirit can be taken away from the unworthy (those who give into the flesh) and so believers must quickly repent if they lapse in their spiritual progress. Origen acknowledged that the Father and the Son are at work in all people and living things, indeed even in nonliving things, but he limited the work of the Spirit to sanctification: "In those persons alone do I think that the operation of the Holy Spirit takes place, who are already turning to a better life, and walking along the way which leads to Jesus Christ, i.e., who are engaged in the performance of good actions, and who abide in God" (I.3.5; 1994, p. 253).

By the middle of the third century, the church had become increasingly institutionalized, partially in response to the need for an authoritative structure to deal with the impact of movements like Montanism and Gnosticism on spiritual practice; and partially because of the increasingly heated theological debates over the relations among God, Christ, the Spirit, the church, and the world. By the end of this century, the charismatic gifts were typically understood to be linked primarily to the office of bishop. Cyprian of Carthage, for example, argued that the gifts of the

Spirit continued after the apostolic age, but that they were reserved for bishops (like himself). Through the desert fathers, who lived lives devoted to solitude and prayer in the wilderness, the understanding of spiritual formation as escape from bodily desire persisted. Yet while the Holy Spirit played a central role in sanctification, the ascetic theologians of this era contributed little to pneumatology per se.

Nicea and the Cappadocians

The situation changed radically in 313 A.D., when persecution of Christians by the Roman State was officially brought to an end. The church found itself in a new political space that permitted opportunities for broader dialogue toward consensus. In fact, the emperor Constantine encouraged the bishops to work out their differences, and sponsored the first ecumenical council. However else one may judge the Constantinian era, it provided a new context within which Christian theology could flourish. Pneumatology began to come into its own in the fourth century.

The Council of Nicea (325 A.D.) was especially concerned with the christological debates over the relation between the Son (or *Logos*) and God the Father. A bishop named Arius had been arguing that God the Father is eternal, but that the *Logos* (which became flesh) was not from eternity; rather, the *Logos* was the first creature, through whom all other things were ordered. Athanasius (293-373 A.D.), bishop of Alexandria, was the primary champion against this view. He was instrumental in the formulation of the Nicene Creed, which insisted that the Son was "of the same substance" *(homoousion)* as the Father.

The third article of the creed, regarding the Holy Spirit, was rather brief: "We believe in the Holy Spirit." It was followed by a reiteration of the condemnation of those who say that the Son is of a different substance. At this stage, christology was the central concern, and questions about the nature and work of the Spirit in relation to the Father, the Son, and the world were left open. After decades of debate in the wake of Nicea, the Council of Constantinople (381 A.D.) would expand the third article of the creed to spell out a clearer understanding of the Spirit: "We believe in the Holy Spirit, the Lord, the Giver of Life, who proceeds from the Father; with the Father and the Son he is worshiped and glorified; he has spoken through the Prophets."

The progress in pneumatology between these two councils was in large part due to the efforts of the three great Cappadocian Fathers of the fourth century: Basil of Caesarea (330-379 A.D.), his younger brother Gregory of Nyssa (335-394), and their comrade Gregory of Nazianzus (329-390). Of course, Athanasius himself continued to play a role in the debates over the divinity of the Spirit. In letters to Bishop Serapion, written around 360, he mentioned that the Spirit, like the Son, is also of the same substance *(homoousion)* with the Father (I.27; 1951, p. 133). However, it was these three theologians from the province of Cappadocia who contributed most significantly to the orthodox formulation of the doctrine of the Holy Spirit.

Like so many creative theological developments, their pneumatological efforts were inspired in part by the need to respond to conflict within the church. The divinity of the Holy Spirit was being explicitly denied by Macedonius, the semi-Arian bishop of Constantinople. He was the leader of a group called the *Pneumatomachoi* (or "fighters of the Spirit"), which was later condemned as heretical. It is important to remember that Nicea had not explicitly affirmed the divinity of the Holy Spirit. As we will see below, the Cappadocians argued for the full equality of the Spirit with the Father and the Son. They maintained the idea that the Father is the eternal Source of the Trinity, but this was not to be taken in a temporal sense; the three persons subsist eternally with and in one another in their distinct relations of origin. God is three persons, but one *ousia* (substance). This trinitarian debate obviously had important implications for the deity of the Holy Spirit, whom the Constantinopolitan creed would insist should be worshiped and glorified along with the other divine persons.

The Cappadocians also had pastoral concerns that fueled their interest in the Spirit. They understood salvation primarily in terms of deification (or *theosis*), the process by which human beings are made to "share in the divine nature" (2 Pet. 1:4). Developing a distinction that would guide Eastern (Greek-speaking) theological discourse on the relation between God and the world, they insisted that deification does not mean that creatures become the same substance as the divine "essence" *(ousia)*, but that they are made to share in the divine "energies" *(energeia)* by which they have fellowship in the divine life. As we will see below, much of Western (Latin-speaking) theology would interpret the God-world relation using different categories, which would contribute significantly to debates over the place of the Spirit in the Trinity. The main point for our purposes here is that the Cappadocians' argument for the deity of the Spirit was bolstered by their understanding of spiritual transformation through deification. Only God can deify creatures. Deification is the work of the Spirit. Therefore, the Spirit must be God.

Although they had much in common, each of the Cappadocians interpreted the transforming experience of the deifying Spirit in unique ways. Basil of Caesarea was in many ways their leader, and is widely regarded as one of the most important players in the patristic development of pneumatology. His writings are characterized by the pastoral concern of a bishop for his flock and filled with reflections on the relation of the Spirit to and in believers. However, his most important contribution to the doctrine is his *De Spiritu Sancto (On the Holy Spirit),* which was written around 375 A.D. (1994). In this work, Basil offers a rigorous exegetical and rhetorical argument for the claim that the Holy Spirit ought to be glorified and adored together with the Father and the Son. His interest is partly liturgical, for he is eager to insist that believers worship the Spirit, whom the Scriptures call "Lord" and to whom they attribute divine qualities (such as omnipresence and saving power).

However, the experience of salvation also has explicit implications for the relations among the persons of the Trinity. Basil teaches that all knowledge of God originates with the Holy Spirit and proceeds through the Son to the Father: "Thus the way of the knowledge of God lies from One Spirit through the One Son to the One Father, and conversely the natural Goodness and the inherent Holiness and the royal Dignity extend from the Father through the Only-begotten to the Spirit" (XXVII.47; 1994, p. 29). According to Basil the Holy Spirit is the life-imparter — the Breath of God who, with the Word, creates and perfects us, granting us a share in the eternal communion of the Trinity. As the bringer of this divine life of intimate fellowship, the Spirit is the very power of God by which (and through whom) we have our life in communion. He spells this out using the imagery of illumination and enlightenment (XXI.52; 1994, p. 34), which will be taken up by later Eastern theologians who will even more strongly emphasize the metaphors of light and energy in relation to the Spirit.

In addition to his description of the personhood of the Spirit, Basil also utilizes the concepts of matter and causality in the development of his pneumatology. He writes of the Father as the original cause, the Son as the creative cause, and the Spirit as the perfecting cause of creation. This works out in a way that is reminiscent of Irenaeus' imagery of the two hands of God: "For the first principle of existing things is One, creating through the Son and perfecting through the Spirit" (XVI.38; 1994, p. 23). Later in the treatise, Basil tackles the difficult issue of the sense in which the Spirit is said to be "in" believers, who are of course embodied. "Form is said to be in Matter; . . . inasmuch as the Holy Spirit perfects rational beings, completing their excellence, He is analogous to Form. For he, who no longer 'lives after the flesh' but, being 'led by the Spirit of God' . . . is described as spiritual" (XXVI.61; 1994, p. 38). This language shows evidence of a more Aristotelian way of conceptualizing the relation between matter and form, demonstrating the relevance of philosophical categories for pneumatology.

Gregory of Nyssa built upon his brother Basil's pneumatological reflections. He too is interested in demonstrating the Spirit's equal glory and divinity with the Father and the Son. In his catechetical (or religiously instructive) efforts, and in various letters, Gregory spelled out in more detail the argument that the Spirit is of the same substance as the Father and the Son. One of his most comprehensive analyses appears in his treatise *On the Holy Spirit*, which is subtitled *Against the Followers of Macedonius*. He insists that the Spirit is of the "same rank" as the Father and the Son, and that "while to be regarded separately in certain distinctive properties, He has in all else . . . an exact identity with them." Gregory argues that Scripture and the Fathers authorize him to declare that the Holy Spirit "is Divine, and absolutely good, and Omnipotent, and wise, and glorious, and eternal" (1994, pp. 315-16). Like Basil he is fond of using metaphors from nature (wind, water, light) to clarify his pneumatological assertions, but images that portray illumination and energy (such as three blazing torches) are the most dominant.

The bishop of Nyssa saw spiritual transformation and trinitarian reflection as intimately implicated in any discussion of the Spirit. It is through the deifying Spirit that we participate in the infinite life of God. Gregory emphasized the ways that this process takes place in the sacraments, especially in baptism, which he defines as "a participation in a life no longer subject to death" (1994, p. 322). It is the Spirit who gives life to baptized believers, and "this life-giving grace should be completed, for those fit to receive it, after starting from that Source [the Father] as from a spring pouring life abundantly, through the Only-begotten Who is the True life, by the operation of the Holy Spirit" (1994, p. 322).

Unlike Origen, however, for whom the Spirit is operative only in believers, Gregory insists that the life-giving, everlasting, essentially-holy

Spirit is "everywhere, being present in each, filling the earth, residing in the heavens, shed abroad upon supernatural Powers, filling all things according to the deserts of each, Himself remaining full, being with all who are worthy, and yet not parted from the Holy Trinity" (1994, p. 323). As essentially related to the Father and the Son, the Holy Spirit is "measureless" and "embraces all things," is "perfect absolutely" and "always beautiful . . . working as He wills all things in all" (1994, pp. 318-20).

In *On Not Three Gods*, Gregory of Nyssa defends the trinitarian language of "three persons in one substance" against the accusation of tritheism. For our purposes, however, the more interesting point is how he emphasizes the Spirit as the "perfecting" divine presence, the gracious power that calls creatures to perfection and holiness in relation to God. The persons all work together, "but every operation which extends from God to the Creation . . . has its origin from the Father, and proceeds through the Son, and is perfected in the Holy Spirit" (1994, p. 334). The power of the Spirit operative within and upon creatures is not interpreted primarily as a determinative force from behind, but as a personal presence that calls them toward participation in the divine life.

Gregory of Nazianzus was bishop of Constantinople for a brief time in 381, but resigned his post shortly after his appointment due to complicated religious and political issues. Sometimes referred to as "Gregory the Theologian" or "Nazianzen," one of his contributions to pneumatology was his emphasis on progressive revelation in his fifth theological oration, "On the Holy Spirit." This made conceptual room for new interpretations of the nature and work of the Holy Spirit. According to Gregory, the Hebrew Bible revealed the Father and alluded to the Son, and the writings of the apostles revealed the Son and alluded to the Spirit. However, this progressive revelation has not ceased, he argues, for "Now the Spirit Himself dwells among us, and supplies us with a clearer demonstration of Himself." He points out that this is what we should expect, since Jesus promised that the Spirit would lead into all truth. Among such truths, argues Gregory, is the recognition of "the Deity of the Spirit Himself." The indwelling, deifying Spirit is the one who brings about "our new creation, and from the new creation our deeper knowledge of the dignity of Him from Whom it is derived" (XXVI–XXVII; 1994, pp. 326-27).

As we noted above, Athanasius was willing to apply the term *homoousion* to the Spirit. In a letter to Count Terentius in the 370s, Basil had urged those who accept that the persons of the Trinity exist in real hypostasis to acknowledge that "the principle of the *homoousion* may be preserved in the unity of the Godhead . . . of Father, Son and Holy Ghost, in the perfect and complete hypostasis of each of the Persons named" (CCXIV.4; 1994, p. 254). Gregory of Nazianzus is equally if not more explicit about the divinity of the Spirit in relation to the other persons of the Trinity. Section X of the oration "On the Holy Spirit" begins in this way: "What then? Is the Spirit God? Most certainly. Well then is He consubstantial? Yes, if He is God" (1994, p. 321). Similarly, in his oration on Holy Baptism, he insists that each of the three persons is "God because Consubstantial," but God is One. Utilizing an increasingly popular image, he observes that "when I contemplate the Three together, I see but one torch, and cannot divide or measure out the Undivided Light" (XV; 1994, p. 375).

Like the other Cappadocians, Nazianzus's argument for the divinity of the Spirit was tied to the experience of divinization by the Spirit. As part of his argument, he restates Athanasius's and Basil's assertion that the Spirit's regenerating power points undoubtedly to the Spirit's full divinity: "For if He is not to be worshipped, how can He deify me by Baptism? But if He is to be worshipped, surely He is an Object of adoration, and if an Object of adoration He must be God" (XXVIII; 1994, p. 327). In his discussion of the three persons and the question of the Unity of God, Gregory upheld both. However, it was his pious commitment to the real divinity of the Spirit that led him to comment: "Better to take a meager view of the Unity than to venture on a complete impiety" (XII; 1994, p. 322). As we will see below, this emphasis on the differentiation in unity of the persons of the Godhead, and the strategy of linking a defense of the deity of the Spirit to the experience of the deifying Spirit, would be emulated throughout the centuries that followed, especially among Greek-speaking theologians.

Although written in the early eighth century, John of Damascus's *Exposition of the Orthodox Faith* summarizes the efforts of the Cappadocians, whom he quotes heavily. Spelling out the fathers' understanding of the third article of the Nicene-Constantinopolitan Creed, he states:

> Likewise we believe also in one Holy Spirit, the Lord and Giver of Life: Who proceedeth from the Father and resteth in the Son; the object of equal adoration and glorification with the Father and Son, since He is co-essential and co-eternal . . . God existing and addressed along with Father and Son: deifying not deified . . . in all things like to the Father and Son: proceeding from the Father and

communicated through the Son, and participated in by all creation, through Himself creating, and investing with essence and sanctifying, and maintaining the universe. (I.8; 1989, p. 9)

Of particular importance here is the language that John uses for the relation between the Spirit and the other persons of the Trinity. The Spirit proceeds from the Father but *rests* on the Son and is communicated *through* the Son. Latin-speaking theologians had developed a different terminology for the intratrinitarian relations. The difference between "the East" and "the West" has certainly been overstated in some historical analyses of the development of the doctrine of the Holy Spirit, but *that* there was a difference can hardly be denied. This difference played a major role in the first major split of the Christian church in 1054 A.D.

The *Filioque* Controversy

As we have seen, the authors of the original Nicene-Constantinopolitan Creed (381 A.D.) confessed belief in the Holy Spirit, "the Lord, the Giver of Life, who proceeds from the Father *(ex Patre)*, who with the Father and the Son together is worshiped and glorified, who spoke by the Prophets." It was common practice throughout Christendom for this creed to be recited during the liturgy. In the Latin-speaking West, however, a new phrase eventually made its way into the spoken creed; the Spirit proceeds from the Father "and the Son" (in Latin, *filioque*). As we will see, it was Augustine (354-430) who set the trajectory for this pneumatological development. As opponents to the *filioque* were quick to point out, such insertions were outlawed by the third ecumenical council, which took place in Ephesus in 431 and forbade any changes to the creed except by a full ecumenical council. In 587, at the Council of Toledo, Spain, Western theologians, sanctioned by the bishop of Rome, officially accepted the addition of the *filioque* phrase into this creed. The ecumenicity of this council was hotly challenged by many Eastern bishops. Nevertheless, most Western Christians confessed each week that the Spirit proceeds from the Father "and the Son."

To the new student of theology, this might seem like a lot of fuss over nothing. As we will see below, however, this aspect of the doctrine of the Holy Spirit continues to be one of the main areas of controversy in the contemporary ecumenical movement; and, indeed, it is far too complex to explain in detail in this context. Our goal in what follows is simply to outline briefly some of the factors that fueled the debate — differences in language, political vision, biblical interpretation, models of salvation, and philosophical categories. Resources for further exploration are described in Part II.

The waxing and waning of the political power of the Roman Empire affected the ability of Western (primarily Latin-speaking) and Eastern (primarily Greek-speaking) Christian theologians to communicate. The relative lack of engagement led to variation among forms of ecclesial life and liturgical practice. Moreover, few theologians were fluent in both languages, which increased the chances of misunderstanding. In the early ninth century, Charlemagne tried to unite the empire again under his rule. When he called for a new council, Pope Leo III attempted to forbid the use of the *filioque* in the creed, but it had already come into wide use and there was great pressure in the West to make it official.

The debate intensified in 858 A.D., as two different political forces vied for authority as bishop in Constantinople; the bishop of Rome installed Ignatius, but the Eastern emperor removed him and put Photius in his place. Like the Cappadocians, Photius was open to the idea that the Spirit proceeded from the Father *through* the Son, but he vigorously attacked the *filioque* for a variety of theological reasons, many of which continue to shape Eastern sensibilities, as we will see below. By 1054, participants on both sides had decided that it was impossible to reconcile their differences and mutual condemnations flew in both directions, splitting the church.

Before we explore some of the philosophical and theological differences, it is important to recognize that both sides appealed to Scripture to support their position. John 15:26 played a central role in the debate: "When the Advocate comes, whom I will send to you from the Father, the Spirit of truth who comes from the Father, he will testify on my behalf." The Spirit of truth "comes from the Father," which supports the original creed. But Jesus also says that he will "send" the Spirit (from the Father), which indicates that the procession of the Spirit also involves the Son. No one denied that Jesus sends the Spirit in the outworking of divine salvation. The question was whether this can also be applied, and if so in what sense, to the inner life of God. In other words, does the Spirit *eternally* proceed from the Son as well as from the Father?

Many Eastern theologians resisted this idea, in part because they wanted to uphold the idea that the Father is the only "source" or "origin" in the Trinity, a doctrine sometimes called monarchianism. At another level, however, there is a question about the appropriateness of applying this particular relation between Jesus and the Spirit in the gospel narratives directly to the eternal nature of God. Scripture also depicts the Spirit as resting on the Son (Mark 1:10; Matt. 3:16; Luke 4:18; cf. Isa. 11:2), and glorifying the Son by taking what is his and declaring it to the world (Jn. 16:14). If Jesus was anointed by and filled with the Spirit in his ministry, ought these characteristics of their relation also be attributed to the inner trinitarian life?

Although the continuities between the East and the West are increasingly emphasized in contemporary theology, it is also important — precisely for the sake of hopeful ecumenical dialogue — to understand the real philosophical and theological differences that led to the emergence and widening of the fissure in the first place. As we argued in the Introduction, assumptions about the nature of matter, personhood, and force are particularly relevant for the development of the doctrine of the Holy Spirit. These interpretive categories shape and are shaped by the experience of salvation by and in the Spirit in particular contexts. In the history of the *filioque* controversy different conceptions of material and immaterial substance, personhood and relation, as well as causality and power played an important role in interpreting the transforming experience of the Spirit.

Let us begin with Augustine, bishop of Hippo in North Africa, generally considered the most influential patristic theologian for the Western tradition. Most scholars agree that the *filioque* controversy originated in, or at least was intensified by, his treatment of the relations among the Father, Son, and the Spirit in his treatise *On the Trinity,* which was completed around 416 A.D. Like most of Augustine's work, this text is motivated by pastoral concern for the transformation of the reader and is couched in prayerful and worshipful recognition of the mystery of God. It is also important to point out that Augustine clearly acknowledges that Christ not only sent the Spirit but also received (and was filled and anointed by) the Spirit (XV.6.46; 1991, p. 431). Moreover, he is in agreement with the Cappadocians when he states, "the source of all godhead, or if you prefer it, of all deity, is the Father. So the Spirit who proceeds from the Father and the Son is traced back, on both counts, to him of whom the Son is born" (IV.5.29; 1991, p. 174). As the *filioque* debate intensified, however, his followers (and detractors) often focused primarily on Augustine's argument for the Spirit's eternal and dual procession from the Father and the Son. In the context of an introduction to the development of pneumatological doctrine, understanding why and how he constructed this argument must be our focus as well.

Augustine appeals to Scripture for his claim that the Spirit proceeds from the Father and from the Son. The Bible refers to the Spirit not only as the Spirit of the Father, but as the "Spirit of Christ" (Rom. 8:9). If the Spirit is referred to as both, then the Spirit proceeds (timelessly) from both (XV.6.45; 1991, p. 430). Augustine takes Jesus' breathing on the disciples and saying "Receive the Holy Spirit" (John 20:22) as a "symbolic demonstration that the Holy Spirit proceeds from the Son as well as from the Father" (IV.5.29; 1991, p. 174). However, he qualifies the dual procession by noting that the Spirit proceeds "principally" from the Father. The Spirit also proceeds from the Son, but "if the Son has everything that he has from the Father, he clearly has from the Father that the Holy Spirit should proceed from him" (XV.6.47; 1991, p. 432).

This interpretation of the Spirit emerges out of Augustine's attempt to explain the compatibility of his belief that God is undivided, incorporeal substance and his belief that God is three persons (or hypostases). The so-called "psychological" analogy is the key to his explanation. Augustine understands the human soul *(psyche)* as comprised of the memory, the intellect, and the will, and yet still one substance. In a similar way, he suggests, we can think of God as one (immaterial) substance, but link the Father with memory, the Son with intellect, and the Spirit with will. This analogy "helps us to see how this three, inseparable in itself, is manifested separately through visible creatures, and how the three are inseparably at work in each of the things which are mentioned as having the proper function of manifesting the Father or the Son or the Holy Spirit" (IV.5.30; 1991, p. 176).

Augustine does recognize the limitations of the analogy, and utilizes a variety of other images and metaphors to depict the relation of the Spirit to the Father and the Son (see below). His main concern throughout is to protect the unity and simplicity of the divine substance, in which the Spirit mysteriously takes his place. Augustine reminds the reader that the human intellect is not able to fully comprehend the nature of God, which is too radiant for us (XV.6.49; 1991, p. 434). Nevertheless, he does privilege the analogy of the human psyche and he does explicitly compare the Holy Spirit to the human will in the culminating chapter of the book (XV.5.38; 1991,

p. 426). Nothing appears to be like the Holy Spirit except our own will (XV.6.41; 1991, p. 427). In the human psyche, it is our will (or love) which bears a likeness to the Holy Spirit (XV.6.43; 1991, p. 428).

It is important to notice the way in which Augustine's anthropological assumptions about the faculties of the human soul impact his doctrine of the Trinity, and so his pneumatology. In his famous debate with his contemporary Pelagius, Augustine is well known for his emphasis on the impotence of the human will, insisting on the total incapacity of the will to choose the good apart from divine grace. Salvation is possible only through a divine work in and transformation of the human will. This divine work is connected, even in *The Trinity*, to the unchangeable "will" of God, which is the "first and the highest cause" of all corporeal species and motion (III.1.9; 1991, p. 132). As we will see, the way in which these voluntaristic and deterministic elements of Augustine's thought were appropriated by later theologians would have implications for the interpretation of the experience of the Holy Spirit.

Augustine placed special emphasis on two terms in relation to the Holy Spirit, *love* and *gift*, both of which are connected to his understanding of the processions within the Trinity. Human *love* provides another analogy for the distinction within the substantial unity of the Trinity in human life, namely, "lover and what is being loved, and love" (VIII.5.14; 1991, p. 255). Reflecting on the Johannine statements that "God is Spirit" (John 4:24) and "God is love" (1 John 4:16), Augustine concludes that while "love" refers first and foremost to the undivided Trinity, the Holy Spirit may be designated as love in a special way. "So it is the Holy Spirit of which he has given us that makes us abide in God and him in us. But this is precisely what love does. He then is the gift of God who is love" (XV.5.31; pp. 420-21). The Holy Spirit is "that by which" the Father and the Son "are joined each to the other." As the bond of love, "the Holy Spirit is something common to Father and Son, whatever it is, or is their very commonness or communion, consubstantial and coeternal. Call this friendship, if it helps, but a better word for it is charity. And this too is substance because God is substance, and God is charity (1 John 4:8, 16), as it is written" (VI.1.7; 1991, pp. 209-10).

The idea that the Holy Spirit is the *gift* of God is also important for Augustine. Here, too, he appeals to Scripture. The Trinity indwells the believer through the gift of God's charity, which has been "poured into our hearts through the Holy Spirit" (Rom. 5:5). Although fully God, the Holy

Spirit may also be spoken of as "the gift of the Father and of the Son. . . . So to signify the communion of them both by a name which applies to them both, the gift of both is called the Holy Spirit" (V.3.12; 1991, p. 197). As with the name "love," the name "gift" is related to Augustine's emphasis on the procession of the Spirit from the Father and the Son. Through the dual procession of the gift of the Holy Spirit, the entire Godhead comes to dwell in us. This gift is the charity which brings us through to God, "without which no other gift of God at all can bring us through to God" (XV.5.32; 1991, p. 421). While Augustine is clear that "love" may be applied within the inner life of the divine persons, this is more ambiguous in the case of the naming of the Spirit as "gift." The tendency to think of the Spirit as "gift" primarily in relation to the "external" saving work of God in the world contributed to the later tendency among some theologians to identify the church with the Spirit.

Among Greek-speaking theologians, the primary theological reason for resisting the *filioque* had to do with their understanding of the monarchy of the Father, which was supported by appeal to Irenaeus's metaphor of the two hands of God, as well as to the Cappadocians, who wrote of the Father's eternal begetting of the Son and breathing of the Spirit. To say the Spirit eternally proceeds from the Father *and* the Son seems to contradict the claim that the Father is the one eternal Source of divinity. However, this concern was also closely tied to the understanding of salvation as deification, which in turn relied on the distinction between "essence" and "energies" in the doctrine of God. As Duncan Reid explains (1997), part of the difference between East and West on this point has to do with differing interpretations of Aristotle's use of the concepts of *ousia* (essence or substance), *dynamis,* and *energeia.* Aristotle's use of these terms was not always consistent. Sometimes he referred to two aspects of a substance *(ousia),* its actuality *(energeia)* and its potentiality *(dynamis);* this was the terminology preferred in the West. At other times he came close to using *energeia* and *dynamis* virtually as synonyms, referring to a substance's energy/power, which is differentiated but not separable from its substance. This usage was taken up and modified in the Eastern doctrine of the divine energies.

We can take Maximus Confessor (580-662 A.D.) as an example. Building on the works of the Cappadocians and others (including the anonymous sixth-century mystical theologian known as Pseudo-Dionysius), he argues that the deification of human nature is the goal of divine creation.

For him the Spirit is central in this process. In *The Church's Mystagogy* he explains that it is only in, by, and through the grace of the Holy Spirit that humans are given "fellowship and identity" with God "by participation in likeness . . . to become God" (XXIV; 1985, p. 207). Yet, as he makes clear in the *Chapters on Knowledge,* this does not mean that humans know God fully, nor that they are changed into the divine substance (essence). This is both because God is "obviously above essence and thought" and because human knowledge is limited. Rather, they know God and participate in God by sharing in the "power" and "act" of God. Like Augustine, Maximus affirms divine simplicity and appeals to mystery to make sense of our experience of the Trinity. Yet the mystery for Maximus is not that there are three persons in the one substance, but that all the persons are fully in one another in the one and the same "essence, power and act of the Father and Son and Holy Spirit" (II.1; 1985, p. 148).

The distinction between the divine essence and the divine energies was further formalized in the work of Gregory of Palamas (1296-1359). The uncreated energy of God is inseparable from the divine essence, but a distinction can still be made. In his *Triads,* Palamas explains that "this mysterious light, inaccessible, immaterial, uncreated, deifying, eternal, this radiance of the divine Nature, this glory of the divinity, this beauty of the heavenly kingdom is at once accessible to sense perception and yet transcends it" (III.1.22; 1983, p. 80). God is not "essential" in the way creatures are, but "Superessential." In other words, the "deifying gift of the Spirit . . . cannot be equated with the super-essential essence of God. It is the deifying energy of this divine essence yet not the totality of this energy, even though it is indivisible in itself" (III.1.34; p. 89). Sharing in the divine energies is really sharing in the divine nature, but does not involve the creature's becoming the essence of God.

Palamas's work was driven in part by his desire to defend a form of spirituality that was highly controversial in the fourteenth-century Orthodox Church. The practice of many "hesychastics" (from the Greek word meaning "stillness" or "silence") involved meditative repetition of a prayer known as the Jesus Prayer, which they claimed led to an intensely transformative vision of God's uncreated light, which the disciples saw at the Transfiguration. In defense of these monks, Palamas insisted that the soul that contemplates the divine life "by the divinizing communion of the Spirit" is glorified, and "made beautiful by the creative and primordial Beauty, and illumined by the radiance of God" (I.3.5; 1983, p. 33). This is a real communion with the divine nature. Spiritual life involves "participating in the inseparable life of the Spirit . . . subsisting in the very nature of the Spirit, Who by nature deifies from all eternity" (III.1.9; 1983, p. 71).

In his exposition of the Eastern use of the idea of divine energies, twentieth-century Eastern Orthodox theologian Vladimir Lossky argues that the Western defense of the *filioque* and resistance to the doctrine of the divinization of creatures go hand in hand (cf. 1985, p. 96). The energies are not "effects" that are foreign to the divine essence, "not acts exterior to God, depending on His will . . . they are *natural* processions of God Himself." This real distinction between the essence and energies implies that God is "more than essence." The divine energies, which "flow eternally" from the divine nature, "being communicated to us by the Holy Spirit, deify us and make us participate in the life of the Holy Trinity" (1985, pp. 54-57). The energies are not to be understood in the sense of effects separate from a cause, but as "manifestations" of the personal reality of God. According to Lossky, the reason the mystical theology of the Eastern church never connects the *eternal* procession of the Son to the mode of intelligence, nor the procession of the Spirit to the mode of the will, is that terms like "wisdom" and "love" are applied only to the energies, "which are subsequent to the essence and are its natural manifestation, but are external to the very being of the Trinity" (1998, p. 81).

Many in the West worried that this implied that God's revelation was not identical to God's being. Some also thought that the Photian view allowed a subordinationism within the Trinity, placing the substantial unity of God in the three persons at risk. For their part, many in the East worried that the *filioque,* and the psychological analogy which supported it, leaned dangerously toward modalism (the doctrine that God was one person with three modes of being). Some also argued that the metaphors of love and gift did not sufficiently uphold the "personhood" of the Holy Spirit. As we have seen, this debate is partly shaped by different ways of construing the ideas of substance (material and immaterial), personhood, and causality. Philosophical shifts in the meaning of these concepts over the centuries have also contributed to the confusion and fueled the controversy. As we will see below, many of the particular pneumatological proposals of the twentieth century, some of which are linked to the broader ecumenical movement, have paid special attention to the way in which such categories influence the task of interpreting the transforming experience of the Spirit of God.

Medieval Mystics and Scholastics

Despite the ongoing debates and mutual condemnations throughout the Middle Ages, creative testimony to the transforming experience of the Holy Spirit would flourish in both the East and the West, although from this point forward we will turn our focus primarily, though not exclusively, to our own Western context. Our interest in this section is pointing to the way in which this doctrine was shaped by two major developments during this period: the growth of mysticism and the emergence of scholasticism. The distinction between a mystic and a scholastic is not clear-cut, and several theologians clearly qualify as both. Generally speaking, however, we can differentiate between descriptions of the Spirit that arise out of intense experiences of contemplation and transformation, and analyses that are primarily oriented toward rational explication of the nature and/or work of the Spirit. Risking oversimplification again, one can observe that mystical treatments of the Spirit are more likely to rely on Platonic or neo-Platonic language, while scholastic treatments increasingly took advantage of the logical and metaphysical apparatus of Aristotle. In this limited space we can only point out a few of the pneumatological formulations from this period, but additional references are provided in Part II (e.g., Richard of St. Victor, Catherine of Siena).

Symeon the "New Theologian" (949-1022), who wrote before the great split between East and West, was well known for his Spirit-centered approach to life and doctrine. This was looked on with suspicion by many of his Byzantine contemporaries, who preferred more rational, Aristotelian methods that de-emphasized personal experience. He was exiled from his post as abbot of St. Mamas in 1009, but continued to write until his death in 1022. In his *Discourses* (1980), a collection of exhortations originally preached to his monks, he devotes seven of thirty-four teachings to the Holy Spirit. Spirit baptism was a central aspect of his pneumatology and spirituality. He wrote that the fullness of the Trinity comes to dwell interiorly in the Christian through the process of cooperation in and with the Holy Spirit, and that this indwelling begins when an individual is baptized in the Holy Spirit. For him the primary evidence of this baptism is the believer's sudden, conscious awareness of the indwelling and deifying life of God. He likens the experience of baptism in the Holy Spirit to immersion in a "pool of light." By this new birth, believers are transformed "from corruptible to incorruptible, from mortal to immortal, from sons of men into

Sons of God and gods by adoption and grace" (XXXII.4; 1980, p. 337). After Spirit baptism, the indwelling of the Trinity is intensified and divine graces increase, leading to increased charity (love) toward neighbors. The "participable and yet incomprehensible" love of God leads one to be "spiritually bound" to others through "holy love in the Holy Spirit" (VIII.2; 1980, pp. 144-45).

Although Anselm, bishop of Canterbury (1033-1109), valued mystical experience and wrote extensively on Christian prayer, he is better known for his rational and argumentative approach to theology. Most of his work focuses on the nature of God or the rational necessity of the Incarnation of the God-Man. When he does treat the Holy Spirit, he is concerned to defend the *filioque* clause against Eastern theologians, rejecting even the idea that the Spirit proceeds from the Father "through" the Son. For the most part, he repeats Augustine's psychological analogies and defends their logical coherence. Yves Congar observes that Anselm "did not develop his pneumatology within the framework of the history of salvation; indeed, he did not refer to the latter at all. . . . Even his prayers and meditations are not pneumatological. They do not even mention the Holy Spirit" (1997, vol. 3, p. 100). Anselm is an important figure in Christian theology for many reasons but his contribution to pneumatology was relatively insignificant.

In contrast, the Cistercian abbot Bernard of Clairvaux (1090-1153) was among those who reacted strongly against rationalistic approaches to interpreting the transformative experience of the Spirit. He preferred the language of passion. Though none of his works focus specifically on the Spirit, throughout his writings he clearly emphasizes the Spirit's role in effecting spiritual union with God in Christ. In his series of sermons on the *Song of Songs* (1987) he builds on Augustine's trinitarian model, allegorically articulating the Spirit in terms of the sensual delights of love: "Surely if the Father kisses and the Son receives the kiss, it is appropriate to think of the Holy Spirit as the kiss, for he is the imperturbable peace of the Father and the Son, their secure bond, their undivided love, their indivisible unity" (VIII.1.2; 1987, p. 237). The intimacy between Father and Son is a "mouth-to-mouth" kiss; a love that surpasses all knowing.

The Bride (a term he uses both of individual believers and of the church) receives the "kiss of the kiss" — the gift of the Spirit, which enables a participation in the pleasurable giving and receiving of the trinitarian life, so that the Bride "understands with love and loves with understanding" (cf. Dreyer, 2001, p. 138). This passionate embrace is the goal of the contemplative life, and Bernard emphasizes that it can and must be pursued with boldness. In fact, it is the Spirit who prompts the Bride to ask audaciously (and trustingly) for a kiss, and it is the Spirit who then becomes her reward as she is taken up into the intimate knowledge and love of God. This rapturous exchange allows for an integration of wisdom and virtue in the Bride, and enables her to reach out in love to her neighbor. Thus in Bernard's mystical thought, the "kiss of the beloved" elicits profound spiritual transformation that gets played out in the lives of both individuals and communities.

The mystic Hildegard of Bingen (1098-1179) was one of the most prominent religious figures of twelfth-century Western Europe. By the end of her life she had become well known as a gifted theologian and prophetic visionary, as well as a talented musician, poet, physician, artist, dramatist, and spiritual director. Hildegard felt called by God and empowered by the Spirit to speak boldly against the corruptions she saw in the political and religious spheres of her day. She influenced popes and princes alike through her extensive traveling, preaching, and writing. Hildegard drew attention to the ways that the Spirit emboldens Christians to carry out the call to speak bravely of God's justice. In her *Scivias,* she writes that the primary purpose of the fiery tongues of Pentecost was to enkindle passionate courage within the disciples so that they would be made "stronger in the name of the Holy and True Trinity" and not retreat from proclaiming God's truth (II.4.1; 1990, p. 190). After the Holy Spirit had "bathed [the disciples] in Its power," they were able to cry out for God's justice in such a way that "the whole world was shaken by their voices" (III.7.7; 1990, p. 415). The Spirit's disturbing presence empowers God's people and uses their voices to convict the world of sin. Hildegard's writing is filled with verdant, fertile, and animated imagery from nature to describe the mysteries of God, and this spills over into her pneumatology (cf. Dreyer, 2001).

Joachim of Fiore (1135-1202) is most well known for his philosophy of history, which is explicitly tied to the doctrine of the Trinity. Based on his reading of the Scriptures and the Latin fathers, Joachim concluded that the inner relations of the trinitarian persons were woven into the very fabric of creaturely time. His writings on the topic are quite complex, and his elaborate and extensive interpretations of the Apocalypse of John and other biblical writings relied heavily on numerological analyses. Broadly speaking, however, he argued that there are three successive (although overlapping) "ages," each correlated with a person of the Trinity. The procession of these ages matched the *filioque* doctrine: The Age of the Father (basically corresponding to Old Testament times) generates the Age of the Son (from New Testament times to Joachim's own era). From both proceeds the Age of the Spirit, which he calculated would begin around 1260. Joachim's tone about the end of the current era was deterministic, but he believed that the new Age of the Spirit would be ushered in by new "Spiritual Men" who would govern the world justly with universal love and spiritual intelligence (cf. Reeves, 1976). The popularity of Joachim's writings contributed to the increase of millenarianism and enthusiasm, as well as drawing new attention to the importance of the doctrine of the Holy Spirit.

In the writings of Bonaventure (1217-1274), the interpretation of the transforming experience of the Spirit takes on a distinctly Franciscan tone, emphasizing the importance of spiritual illumination and love for others. In *The Soul's Journey into God*, he discusses the stages of the ascent of the soul, which involve contemplation and the infusion of divine light, which illuminates the soul and brings it into unity with the goodness and beauty of God. Bonaventure spells out this coming to union in a way that attends to the relations among the Father, Son, and Spirit. In his more explicit treatments of the doctrine of the Trinity, he usually follows Augustine's psychological analogy between the human individual and the being of God. Both are interpreted in terms of the faculties of memory, intellect, and will, which he takes to be consubstantial and interpenetrating one another. These faculties in us lead us to understand the "most blessed Trinity in view of their order, origin and interrelatedness." Intelligence comes forth from memory as its offspring, and "from memory and intelligence love is breathed forth as their mutual bond" (III.5; 1978, p. 84).

By the thirteenth century, several of Aristotle's works that had been lost to the West came into circulation through dialogue with Arab philosophers. The coherence and logical rigor of his system contributed significantly to the founding and structuring of European universities. The term "high scholasticism" is sometimes used to refer to this era, during which theology was often treated as the "queen of the sciences." Christian theologians were confronted with the task of interpreting the experience of the Spirit in dialogue with Aristotle's vision of the cosmos and of the human person, both of which quickly came to dominate Western culture.

The most well-known and influential medieval scholastic theologian was Thomas Aquinas (1225-1274). Like most of his predecessors Thomas's pneumatology is anchored in his view of the Trinity. Building on Augustine's psychological analogy, he agrees that there are two eternal processions in God, which can be understood on the model of the faculties of thinking and willing in the individual human soul. The Word, or the Son, proceeds eternally by mode of intellectual understanding from the Father, whereas the Spirit proceeds eternally by mode of will or love from the Father and from the Son as from one principle (*Summa Theologiae*, I.36.3, 4).[2] Because God's essence is simple (that is, without division or potential for change like material essences), the divine intellect cannot be thought of as substantially different from the divine will. Nevertheless, Thomas makes a distinction on the basis of relations of origin. Although these processions are one in God, we can speak of a logical ordering. The first procession (of the Word) is properly called "generation," and the second procession (of the Spirit) is properly named "spiration." This logical priority of *logos* over *pneuma* is in part supported by appeal to the ordering of the faculties of the human soul, in which the procession of love (will) follows the procession of the intellect, "since nothing can be loved by the will unless it is conceived in the intellect" (*ST*, I.27.3).

Thomas does not simply repeat Augustine's pneumatology, however, but refigures it in light of his appropriation of Aristotelian philosophy. As we noted in the Introduction, the latter interpreted the movement of all things in terms of their formation (or actualization) toward their proper goal. The ultimate "final" cause of the movement of rational souls was God as the unmoved mover, thought thinking itself as the perfect Good, toward which all intellectual activity is oriented as its proper *telos*, or goal. Thomas was interested in interpreting the Christian experience of redemptive transformation in relation to the Good in a way that both accommodated the biblical differentiation between the Father, Son, and Spirit, and upheld the perfect unity of the divine substance. Insisting that all the external acts of God in relation to creation are undivided, he nevertheless emphasizes the role of the Holy Spirit in the creaturely longing for the Good, which is spelled out in terms of final causality.

The orientation of human hope toward the future is conditioned by the creative presence of the Spirit. "[H]ope of obtaining the end arises

---

2. There are many available editions of Thomas Aquinas's *Summa Theologiae*, so when quoting this work we will use the standard scholarly format only, so that readers may consult any one they like.

from the fact that something is moving in the right way towards the end, and drawing close to it. . . . But the Holy Spirit brings one to the end, and the Gifts perfect us for obeying and following him" (*ST,* I-II.69.1). For Thomas, believers are enabled to grow in their moral lives toward the ultimate end of the beatific vision of God through the gifts and fruit of the Spirit (*ST,* I-II.68, 70). Linking the Spirit to final causality also provides Thomas with a way of emphasizing that the Spirit is present not only in human beings, but throughout creation, enlivening all things and moving them toward the particular (good) *telos* for which they were created. As he puts in his *Compendium Theologiae:* "It was suitable that the effects of divine Providence should be situated close to the Holy Spirit, since the whole of divine government is dependent on divine goodness, which is appropriated to the Holy Spirit, who proceeds as love" (Cf. Congar, 1997, vol. 3, p. 122).

When Thomas comes to treat the doctrine of the *filioque,* he not only defends its coherence but argues that it is necessary for the proper articulation of the mystery of the One God as Father, Son, and Holy Spirit. If Son and Spirit did not differ in the order of their origin — that is, by the distinctness of their relations — they would be indistinguishable from each other and God would not be Trinity but rather Dyad (*ST,* I.36.2; cf. *Summa Contra Gentiles,* IV.4, 24). In his logical explication of these distinctions, which are not to be taken as "real" in a way that would divide the divine substance, he builds upon and reinforces Augustine's naming of the Spirit as Love and Gift (*ST,* I.37, 38) and as the bond of love between the Father and the Son (*ST,* I.36.4, 37.1, 39.8).

At one point it appears that Thomas is willing to accept the equivalence of the *filioque* with the idea, sponsored by many of the Greek fathers, that the Spirit proceeds from the Father *through* the Son (*per filium* in Latin). He argues that since "the Holy Spirit proceeds from the Son as from the Father, it is acceptable to say, 'The Father spirates the Holy Spirit through the Son,' or, what comes to the same thing, 'The Holy Spirit proceeds from the Father through the Son'" (*ST,* I.36.3). In the response to objections, he adds: "If, however, we look to the persons spirating, then we find that even though the Holy Spirit proceeds from the Father together with the Son, he proceeds from the Father immediately, for he is from the Father, but also mediately, inasmuch as he is from the Son." What would worry many Eastern theologians was not so much this notion of mediation, but Thomas's argument in the next article that "just as Father and

Son are the one God because of the unity of the form signified by the name 'God,' so also they are the one principle of the Holy Spirit because of the unity of the property signified in the term 'principle'" (*ST,* I.36.4). Here the metaphor of the two hands of God is replaced by an image of the Spirit as proceeding from the one causal principle called "Father and Son."

Most Western medieval scholastic theologians followed Thomas (and Augustine) in connecting the divine intellect to the Son, and the divine will to the Spirit. This meant that they also inherited the conceptual difficulties that came with this approach, such as its apparent incompatibility with divine simplicity. If there are "real" relational distinctions between the Spirit, the Son, and the Father in God, then the divine substance seems to be divisible. In the Aristotelian system, being divisible and being changeable (having "potentiality") were linked; theologians who followed this logic would insist that the unchangeable God must be pure "actuality." Duns Scotus (d. 1308) tried to solve the problem with his notion of "formal" distinctions between the divine essence, intellect, and will. God's intellect is infinite and perfect, and from it there issues a love proportionate to this infinite perfection — the Holy Spirit. These two faculties, intellect and will, are the only productive principles in God, argued Scotus, and so it follows logically that there can only be two productions, the Word and the Spirit.

William of Ockham (1288-1348), on the other hand, argued that there are no real *or* formal distinctions between essence, intellect, and will in God; these terms are merely "names" that we use to make sense of our particular experiences. He concluded that the Trinity is a concept that can only be accepted by faith and not by reason. His "nominalism" would play an important role in the rise of modern science. Already by the end of the fourteenth century, however, social and religious changes were beginning to occur that would radically alter the structure of the ongoing Christian dialogue about the nature and work of the Holy Spirit.

The Protestant Reformation

Recent scholarship on the Protestant Reformation commonly distinguishes between the "magisterial" reformers, who tried to work within the existing ecclesial structures or develop new ones that were specially connected to kings or princes or the state, and the "radical" reformers, who re-

sisted forms of the church that were too closely conne[...]
its power. Both forms of Protestantism are still with us[...]
represented by those traditions influenced especially[...]
and Zwingli (such as the European state churches) and[...]
tions like the Anabaptist peace churches, influenced[...]
Menno Simons.

Much of the theological energy of early Reform[...]
magisterial and radical, was devoted to critical engage[...]
Catholic formulations and practices related to the do[...]
What is the relation between the natural human wi[...]
works) and the divine will (and power) to save by gra[...]
estant theology was so focused on articulating and de[...]
trine of justification by faith, many other doctrines, suc[...]
Trinity and the Spirit, did not initially receive as much[...]
way in which the Holy Spirit was understood and experie[...]
clearly shaped the debates over justification, even when[...]
made explicit.

The figure most commonly associated with what later[...]
called the Protestant Reformation was Martin Luther (d. 154[...]
ways Luther was still a late medieval theologian; many of the[...]
with which he worked were explicitly Augustinian, which is not[...]
since he was an Augustinian monk. In his explication of the third[...]
the creed in the *Smaller Catechism*, he emphasizes that by o[...]
strength or reason it is impossible to come to Christ. The good n[...]
Luther is that "the Holy Spirit has called me through the Gospel, e[...]
ened me with his gifts, and sanctified and preserved me in true fait[...]
as he calls, gathers, enlightens, and sanctifies the whole Christian ch[...]
on earth and preserves it in union with Jesus Christ in the one true f[...]
(1959, p. 345). For the most part Luther followed Augustinian pattern[...]
his formal presentations of the doctrine of the Trinity and the Holy Spi[...]
Moreover, Luther seemed at times to downplay the role of the Spirit in h[...]
polemics with the enthusiasts. This led to a consensus among Luthe[...]
scholars that pneumatology was not central to his theology, and that he[...]
made no special contribution to this doctrine.

This reading of Luther was challenged in the twentieth century by[...]
Danish theologian Regin Prenter in his book *Spiritus Creator: Luther's[...]
Concept of the Holy Spirit*. He argued that pneumatology played a much[...]
more important role in Luther's theology than scholars had previously[...]

ized. In fact, Prenter begins with the claim that "the concept of the
pirit completely dominates Luther's theology" (1953, p. ix). The cre-
work of the Spirit, which involves both annihilation as well as vivifi-
, is understood by Luther as the real, personal, eschatological pres-
of God in the world. Prenter argues that Luther's theology is aimed
st rationalist and idealist notions of the Spirit, which he found in so
y medieval writers. For Luther "the Holy Spirit is a real and divine
re of revelation in which the risen Christ alone is present as a present
redeeming reality" (p. 61). This "sphere" not only illumines the intel-
but transforms the whole person and indeed the whole church and the
ole cosmos. For Luther the Holy Spirit is not a "transcendent causality"
t "the living and acting God himself who draws us into his all-
bracing, eschatological, saving act" (p. 171).

This gracious act of God as *Spiritus Creator* incorporates and em-
races what we distinguish as the works of creation, redemption, justifica-
on, and sanctification. For example, in the response to Erasmus in *The
Bondage of the Will*, Luther consistently speaks of the role of the Spirit in
the gracious calling and justification of sinners. The human will is not free
to believe or move toward God, for this is wholly the gift of the Spirit, who
lives in and moves those who are drawn by the Father, whose shedding
abroad of the Spirit enlightens the ungodly by displaying and making
Christ present. In fact, Luther insists that even if his opponents "will not
own themselves beaten and come over to my view, or be silent," it is not in
his power to force them; this too must be "the gift of the Spirit of God"
(2003, p. 299). Like Augustine, Thomas, and others, Luther did not divide
the works of God in relation to creation among the persons of the Trinity,
so the all-encompassing act of *Spiritus Creator* must be understood not as
the work of the Spirit alone but as the work of the Spirit poured out by the
Father who draws us into union with the Son.

To understand why Luther was tempted to downplay the role of the
Spirit in some of his polemical writings, it is necessary to understand the
context of his debates with the "enthusiasts." In their enthusiasm for
Spirit-led living among laypersons, some radical reformers rejected the hierarchy of the established church, refusing to rely on the clergy for interpreting the Scripture and the administration of the sacraments. One of
Luther's most fiery antagonists was Thomas Müntzer, whom he colorfully
depicted as a representative of Satan. For his part, Müntzer returned the
rhetorical barbs, referring to Luther as "Doctor Liar." His view of Luther's

spirituality is reflected even in the subtitle of his treatise "Vindication and Refutation: A Highly Provoked Vindication and Refutation of the unspiritual soft-living Flesh in Wittenberg, whose robbery and distortion of Scripture has so grievously polluted our wretched Christian Church" (Müntzer, 1988, p. 327). Rejecting the need for academic learning in interpreting Scripture, Müntzer appealed directly to the testimony of the Spirit.

In the larger version of his *Prague Manifesto* he declared "freely and frankly that I have never heard any donkey-farting doctor whisper the tiniest fraction or slightest point about the order [established in God and all creatures]" and insisted that only by receiving the Holy Spirit, who gives an "invincible testimony," can God be understood (1988, p. 363). Müntzer believed that the Spirit had filled him with special power as the "new Daniel," and that along with his followers, whom he viewed as the elect, he was called in the "last days" to use the sword against any who refused to participate in the true reformation of the world. Worldly princes, like Nebuchadnezzar of old, ought to listen to his prophetic utterances, which were direct instructions from the Holy Spirit (cf. Burgess, vol. 3, p. 208). He was often accused of inciting riots and revolution against the state and the church that had accommodated itself to the world. This "enthusiasm" was worrisome to Martin Luther, among others, not only for political reasons, of course, but also because it challenged the relation between the Spirit and the Word.

Pneumatology also played an important role in Luther's battle with other magisterial reformers, especially with Huldrych Zwingli over the nature of the sacraments. Zwingli accepted only the Lord's Supper and baptism as sacraments, because they alone were instituted by Christ. However, he rejected the doctrine of the real presence of Christ in the Supper and the real (instrumental) saving power of the water in baptism. This is tied to his understanding of the Holy Spirit. He believed that at Pentecost the Spirit came in place of Christ, after the latter's resurrection and ascension, guiding the church until his return. This means that Christ's body is not "really" present on earth, not even in the sacraments, but only "symbolically" present. Real transformation occurs through the presence of the Spirit, but this is not tied to the elements of the Supper or baptism, but to internal spiritual renewal, which is wholly dependent on the gracious will of God. Zwingli was more willing than Luther to acknowledge that Scripture can only be rightly interpreted through the special gifts of the Spirit, who helps the reader understand beyond the literal meaning of the text.

Luther called him a *Schwärmer,* or enthusiast, for this reason, but Zwingli's pneumatological writings and practices have led some scholars to call *him* the "theologian of the Holy Spirit" (cf. Burgess, vol. 3, p. 159).

We can spell out Luther's distinction from these opponents in three general areas (cf. Prenter, 1953, pp. 299-301). The first has to do with debates over the Lord's Supper. The enthusiasts called for a spirituality that did not require attending to the real presence of Christ and the hearing of the Word, but which, he thought, focused only on the Spirit to the exclusion of the flesh. Luther aimed to hold the two together radically; the Supper has a real bodily effect. The second area concerns Luther's understanding of the spiritual life. He accused the enthusiasts of a false spiritualism that attempted to escape the lowliness of the embodied Christ and escape to a "higher" and "naked" experience of the Spirit. Luther aimed to hold together Word and Spirit absolutely. His view of the Incarnation, similarly, was one that embraced the union of the divine nature and the human flesh wholly. So true spirituality is really embodied, made possible by the Spirit's empowering of persons in real ethical and social contexts. Third, Luther, for all his antagonism toward the Roman Catholic Church, still believed that Christ is made present to us by the Spirit in the church. He saw the enthusiasts' resistance to engaging in church fellowship as rejecting the outward, public signs of revelation, while he wanted to insist that it is through these that the Spirit does his hidden sanctifying work.

While many of the early radical reformers (like Müntzer) were violent and apocalyptic, other participants in this tradition insisted that the kingdom of God would be established through peaceful means. Menno Simons (1496-1561) is a prime example, and is considered the founder of the Mennonites. Simons's doctrine of the Holy Spirit was basically orthodox, following the traditional emphasis on the deity of the Spirit as the third person of the Trinity. One of the distinctive elements of this tradition, linked to the name Anabaptists (literally "re-baptizers"), is the belief that water baptism itself does not save, but only baptism with or in the Spirit, who sanctifies and leads into truth. Simons had been a Catholic priest, but came to believe that the idea that the substance of an infant's soul is regenerated through the waters of baptism was unbiblical and hurtful to Christian life. He appealed, for example, to Acts 10:47-48, where Peter calls for the water baptism of those who had already received the Holy Spirit (1966, p. 276). Water baptism is a sign of faith and obedience, but regeneration occurs through the renewing power of the Holy Spirit. In response to his persecutors, Simons insists that they do indeed "desire a right Christian baptism; first, with Spirit and fire . . . and afterwards in water" (1966, p. 304). So Simons advocated the rebaptism of many who had been baptized as infants.

John Calvin (1509-1564), one of the most influential theologians in the Reformed tradition, was quite critical of the Anabaptists, partly because of his desire, shared by Luther, to uphold the importance of traditional sacramental practices (if not traditional sacramental interpretations) for the sake of ecclesial order. Also like Luther, Calvin tended to follow the basic Augustinian-Thomist vision of the relation of the Spirit to the Father and the Son. Although he is somewhat suspicious of philosophical terms such as substance, hypostasis, and *homoousion,* in his *Institutes of the Christian Religion* he acknowledges their importance and usefulness for upholding and clarifying the orthodox trinitarian interpretation of Scripture. Along with most of the Western tradition, he writes of the Father as the fountain and wellspring of all, the Son as wisdom or ordered disposition, and the Spirit as the power and efficacy of divine action. Calvin also accepts a modified form of faculty psychology, which is taken into his doctrine of humanity as the image of God. Thus it is not surprising that he affirms the *filioque,* acknowledging a logical order within the eternal divine life: "the Father is thought of as first, then from him the Son, and finally from both the Spirit" (*Inst.* I.13.18-19).[3]

"Calvinist" theology is often stereotyped as rigidly deterministic and rationalistic, focused on the order of the *Logos* rather than the dynamism of the Spirit. A review of Reformed theology over the centuries suggests that this judgment is not wholly unwarranted. However, on the occasion of the celebration of Calvin's four-hundredth birthday, Princeton theologian Benjamin B. Warfield argued that Calvin's pneumatology might be his most significant gift to the church. "Calvin's greatest contribution to theological science lies in the rich development which he gives — and which he was the first to give — to the doctrine of the work of the Holy Spirit . . . we must say that the doctrine of the work of the Holy Spirit is a gift from Calvin to the Church . . . In his hands, for the first time in the history of the Church, the doctrine of the Holy Spirit comes to its rights . . . above everything else he deserves, therefore, the great name of *the theologian of the Holy Spirit*" (Warfield, 1974, pp. 485-87, emphasis in original).

---

3. There are many available editions of Calvin's *Institutes,* so here too we will employ only the standard scholarly format. In Part II of this book we include a well-known edition.

As we have seen, in his formal treatment of the doctrine of the Trinity, Calvin did not do much more than repeat the Augustinian formulations. His major pneumatological contribution lies elsewhere, in his interpretation of the transforming experience of the Spirit, especially in Book III of the *Institutes*. His whole doctrine of salvation is pneumatologically mediated. Chapter 1 of Book III bears the title "The things spoken concerning Christ profit us by the secret working of the Spirit," and begins with a depiction of the Holy Spirit "as the bond that unites us to Christ." We come to enjoy Christ and all his benefits through the "secret energy of the Spirit," whose principal work is the creation of faith in believers, binding them to Christ. "Until our minds become intent upon the Spirit, Christ, so to speak, lies idle because we coldly contemplate him as outside ourselves — indeed far from us" (III.1.3). It is through the Holy Spirit that knowledge of God in Christ is revealed to our minds and sealed upon our hearts (III.2.7).

For Calvin the main task of the doctrine of salvation is not figuring out the order of justification and sanctification but tending to the presence of the Holy Spirit within which all redemptive transformation occurs. Calvin's *Commentaries* also provide ample evidence of his interest in the role of the Holy Spirit in our salvific knowledge of and union with God in Christ. For example, in his commentary on 1 Corinthians 1:8-9, he insists that it is the Spirit alone who is a faithful and sure witness to the believer that he or she is confirmed in Christ. Discussing the text in Galatians 2:20, which speaks of being crucified with Christ, Calvin interprets this in terms of "becoming one with Christ," by which he means a life spent partaking in Christ's righteousness and being governed by the Spirit. And in explaining the mystery of Christ's being united to the church in Ephesians 5:32, he argues that "here the infinite power of the Divine Spirit is exerted."

We could also point to some of the differences between Luther and Calvin by demonstrating their preference for Aristotle and Plato, respectively, but for the sake of this introductory text we will conclude by observing some of their similarities. For both reformers the experience of justification by faith is understood as a union with Christ that is inextricable from a transforming experience of the Spirit of God. As we have seen, both worried about individuals who claimed to have a special revelation from the Holy Spirit that led or contributed to disorderly behavior, which was connected to their high view of the sacraments and the church. Both were in many ways late medieval theologians, operating still within an astrological, elemental, and geocentric view of the world, a view that would soon collapse under the challenges of modern science.

Perhaps more than anything else, however, these magisterial reformers were united, along with the radical reformers, in their protest against the self-understanding and political practices of the Roman Catholic Church, which presupposed and reinforced a particular way of linking the Spirit with the mother church. As with the split between East and West in 1054, debates over pneumatology played an important role in the separation of the Protestants from the Roman Catholic Church.

The Catholic Reformation

The sixteenth-century reforms from within the Roman Catholic Church were not simply a reaction to the emergence of Protestantism; they were also driven by widespread internal concerns about abuses of power and by doctrinal disputes. For this reason scholars are increasingly referring to these developments as the "Catholic Reformation" rather than the "Counter-Reformation," although the student of this period will often find the latter phrase in earlier historical treatments. Some Catholic reformers were focused on the clarification of traditional Christian doctrine, not only for polemical purposes in debate with the Protestants, but also for the sake of holding together the monastic orders and theological factions wavering in their commitment to the authority of Rome. Other Catholic reformers put their energy into the clarification and restoration of spiritual practices in order to facilitate the renewal of healthy personal and communal life within the church. In this section, we will briefly explore examples of both of these modes of reformation. Although we might point to several others, Ignatius of Loyola and John of the Cross will serve as our primary illustrations of the renewed focus on contemplative practice.

First, however, let us briefly describe the treatment of the Holy Spirit in the Council of Trent, which met intermittently from 1545-1563 and represents by far the most significant contribution to the struggle for doctrinal clarification in the Roman Catholic Church during this era. Trent was explicitly concerned with strengthening church discipline and administration in response to both corruption among the clergy and the growing pluralism that flourished after the Renaissance. The decisions of the council were divided into decrees, which contained positive statements of Roman dogma, and canons, which condemned those with dissenting views as "anathema." After affirming the Nicene-Constantinopolitan Creed, the Council acknowledged the Apocrypha as part of the biblical canon and decreed that no one is allowed to interpret the Scripture in a way that is contrary to the sense held by the "holy mother Church." The meaning and proper administration of the sacraments received the most attention in the decrees. Very little was written about the Holy Spirit, and none of it new. Yet this is understandable; the purpose of Trent was not to advance new formulations of doctrine, but to clarify the traditional teachings of the church (cf. Ganoczy, 1979, p. 55).

One of the early decrees of Trent deals explicitly with the doctrine of justification, partially in response to Luther's harsh criticism of the Roman teaching on salvation and the practice of indulgences. Luther had insisted that salvation is by grace alone, through faith alone, understood through Scripture alone, mediated through *Christ alone*. It is precisely here that the theologians of Trent emphasized the role of the Holy Spirit in salvation. Canon XI of the sixth session (on justification) anathematizes anyone who says that we are justified "either by the sole imputation of the justice of Christ, or by the sole remission of sins, to the exclusion of the grace and the charity which is poured forth in their hearts by the Holy Ghost, and is inherent in them." Much could be said about this debate, but let us focus in this context on the implications for pneumatology. It is significant that the Roman response to Protestant christocentrism points to the importance of the transforming grace and love of the Holy Spirit in believers.

In Chapter V of the sixth session, the Council clearly states that an individual cannot move by his or her own free will, without the grace of God, toward justification. The prevenient grace of God is the beginning of the process, but when "God touches the heart of man [*sic*] by the illumination of the Holy Ghost," that person can reject or cooperate with this grace. The Spirit is understood here and elsewhere in the Council as awakening human persons, inviting them to participate in and cooperate with God's justifying grace. In Chapter VII of the same session, the Council uses neo-Aristotelian categories to describe the causes of justification. The final cause is the glory of God, the instrumental cause is the sacraments, and the meritorious cause is the death of Christ. The efficient cause, however, is the merciful God who graciously washes, sanctifies, signs, and anoints "with the Holy Spirit of promise."

Besides the doctrine of justification, and occasional references in the decrees on the sacraments, the Council's treatment of the Spirit was for the most part focused on the relation between the Spirit and the authority of the church. The same Spirit that inspired Scripture inspires the holy mother church. This means that the church has exclusive authority to interpret Scripture through its traditional formulations, including Trent's own decrees. As Yves Congar explains: "[W]hereas the Reformers attributed [scriptural] interpretation to the Holy Spirit, the theologians of Trent ascribed it to 'the Church,' since it was, they believed, in the Church that the Spirit was living, the Church itself that was the living gospel" (1997, p. 153). Although pneumatology was not an explicit focus in the Council of Trent, it is clear that differences in the way in which Roman and Protestant theologians understood the Holy Spirit played a significant role in their mutual condemnations, as well as in their respective efforts at reformation.

Much of the creative work on interpreting the transforming experience of the Spirit occurred outside the council meetings of Trent. Many of the contemplatives during this period, at work in monasteries or active in other forms of service, were more interested in facilitating the reformation of personal and communal spiritual practices than in the debates over the causes of justification. Here too, however, theological decisions about the work of the Holy Spirit in relation to the church and the individual soul registered a profound effect in their writings about sanctification and transformation.

One of the most well-known contemplative theologians associated with the Catholic Reformation was Ignatius of Loyola (1491-1556), who was the founder of the Society of Jesus, or the Jesuits. The concern of this Spanish mystic and reformer for spiritual discipline and renewal of the church is clear in his *Spiritual Diary*. Although he does not explicitly develop a pneumatology, he refers to the Holy Spirit in the context of his trinitarian reflection on mystical experience. "I will think over what I ought to say to the Three Divine Persons." He prays: "Eternal Father, confirm me! Eternal Son, confirm me. Eternal Holy Spirit, confirm me. Holy Trinity, confirm me. My One and Only God, confirm me" (I.3.48; 1991, pp. 244-45). He also describes intense divine visitations wherein he became aware of the Spirit's movement and "procession" from the divine essence (which he saw as taking place from the Father and the Son, according to the standard Western view). At one point in the *Diary*, he indicates that in preparation for Mass he "perceived or saw the Holy Spirit himself. Everything was affectionate awe" (II.6.169; 1991, p. 262). However, as the naming of his Society suggests, his spiritual practices are oriented more toward contemplating and ordering one's life in accordance with the way of Jesus.

Ignatius is radically devoted to the holy mother church, whose Spirit-inspired authority he takes as absolute. In the *Spiritual Exercises,* he calls his followers to emulate his total submission to the church. "What I see as white, I will believe to be black if the hierarchical Church thus determines it. For we believe that between Christ our Lord, the Bridegroom, and the Church, his Spouse, there is the one same Spirit who governs and guides us for the salvation of our souls. For it is by the same Spirit and Lord of ours who gave the Ten Commandments that our holy Mother Church is guided and governed" (§365; 1991, p. 213). This way of linking the Spirit and the church was challenged by Protestant reformers of all types. For our purposes, the main point is that underlying the political and social conflicts and the debates over biblical interpretation were significant differences in the way in which the parties interpreted the transforming experience of the Holy Spirit.

John of the Cross (1542-1591) was another sixteenth-century Spanish mystic and reformer, perhaps best known for his work *Dark Night of the Soul.* Like Ignatius, he is careful to reaffirm traditional formulations of the relation of the Spirit to the other persons of the Trinity. For example, he follows the Augustinian analogy (refigured by Bonaventure) between the substantial faculties of the human soul (memory, intellect, and will) and the three members of the Trinity (Father, Son, and Spirit). His primary interest, however, is not in doctrinal clarification but in testifying to and facilitating mystical experiences that transform the soul through union with God. The delights of spiritual union with God are only possible on the other side of purgative experiences, which he describes with terms like "negation," "void," and "utter darkness." In "nakedness and poverty of spirit," the soul is stripped of all "faculties, passions, appetites, and affections" so that it "no longer loves in a lowly manner, with its natural strength, but with the strength and purity of the Holy Spirit" (II.4.2; 1987, p. 200).

In *The Living Flame of Love* (1987), John writes of the Spirit as the fire in which the soul is consumed and transformed. The Spirit is the vibrant flame that flares up within the soul who is being united with God.

O sweet cautery,
O delightful wound!
O gentle hand!
O delicate touch
that tastes of eternal life
And pays every debt!
In killing you changed death to life. (II.1; 1987, p. 303)

John explicitly correlates the Spirit to the cautery, the Father with the hand, and the Son with the touch, although he emphasizes that they are substantially the same and the divine work is united. For our purposes, the interesting point is that in the experience of transformation John begins with the Holy Spirit.

The intense experience of the transforming Spirit was so delightful for John that he often used the imagery of a love affair to describe it. In his *Spiritual Canticle,* a poem based on the biblical Song of Songs, he writes of the longing that draws the Bride (the individual soul) and the Bridegroom (God) toward each other. This desirous exchange is fueled by the Holy Spirit, who "intervenes to effect this spiritual union" by cultivating qualities of "purity, fortitude, and love" in the soul. He writes of the Holy Spirit as the "divine breath-like spiration" that elevates the soul and "makes her capable of breathing in God the same spiration of love that the Father breathes in the Son and the Son in the Father, which is the Holy Spirit Himself, who in the Father and the Son breathes out to her in this transformation, in order to unite her to himself" (XXXIX.3; 1987, p. 280). The unifying consummation between the lovers comes about by the transformation of the soul in the lively and burning flame of the Holy Spirit in which there is a "beatific conformity and satisfaction of both lover and beloved" (XXXIX.14; 1987, p. 282).

The doctrinal clarification of the Council of Trent and the spiritual reforms of contemplative theologians like Ignatius of Loyola and John of the Cross had a profound influence on Roman Catholicism, and these developments continue to register an effect today. Pneumatology, however, was rarely an explicit theme for these reformers. As we will see below, in the twentieth century many Roman Catholic theologians did turn their attention to the doctrine of the Holy Spirit, notably at the Second Vatican Council. This renewal has in part been fueled by the recognition that Catholic theology in the centuries following Trent suffered from an insufficiently robust pneumatology. In his trilogy on the Holy Spirit, Roman Catholic theologian Yves Congar makes this observation about this phase of reflection on the doctrine: "At that time, the Spirit was seen, on the one hand, as the principle of holy living in the souls of individuals — this was the 'internal mission' — and, on the other, as guaranteeing acts of the institution, especially its infallible teaching. This certainly does not constitute a pneumatology" (1997, vol. 1, p. 156). A similarly harsh assessment has often been made by twentieth-century Protestant theologians about the treatment of the Holy Spirit in their own traditions.

Early and Late Modern Interpretations

Protestant Scholasticism and Pietism

The term "Protestant Scholastics" generally refers to seventeenth- and eighteenth-century Lutheran and Reformed theologians who defended and clarified the doctrinal formulations of their relatively new traditions in debate with Roman Catholic theologians and with one another. For the most part, these theologians relied on primarily Aristotelian logical categories as they outlined rational arguments for their doctrinal assertions. The more ambiguous label "Pietist," on the other hand, often refers to specific historical movements, but in this context we simply mean to indicate theologians (they were often also pastors) who were more or less unhappy with the rationalistic approach of the scholastics, which they attempted to balance by attending to the formation of religious affections and spiritual practices. Although many Protestant theologians, pastors, and evangelists during this period treated the Holy Spirit in their writings (e.g., Jeremy Taylor, 1990), we will limit ourselves in this section to exploring general tendencies among the scholastics and pietists (broadly understood). The theological efforts of both types of Protestant theologians were shaped in part by the rise of early modern science, which increasingly challenged the philosophical categories that had dominated theological discourse during the Middle Ages.

As we noted in the Introduction, Christian theology emerged during an era shaped by the philosophical categories of Middle Platonism, which incorporated aspects of the work of Plato, Aristotle, and the Stoics. By the early modern period, Roman Catholic theology had become heavily reliant on Aristotelian categories. At the same time, philosophers like René Descartes were reviving Platonic emphases, especially the dualism between material and immaterial substance. And the individualistic tendencies of Stoicism were increasingly being appropriated in early modern anthropology and political philosophy. The rise of modern science during this period also led to the growth in popularity of the more materialistic physics of the Stoics. The laws of classical mechanics were expressed in terms that had much more in common with the atomism and determinism of Stoic philosophy. Isaac Newton himself wanted to hold on to some form of final causality, but the explanatory power of mechanistic (efficient) causality eventually led to astronomer Pierre-Simon LaPlace's infamous claim that he had no need for the hypothesis "God" to make sense of movement in the universe.

This was the context within which these Christian theologians struggled to articulate the way in which the divine Spirit registers a transformative effect on human life. The work of the Protestant scholastics engaged the categories of all three "schools" of philosophy in their polemics against the Roman Catholics and against materialistic science. They were more comfortable using the Aristotelian categories of the medieval period than were the early Reformers like Luther and Calvin, but their propositions about the relation of the Holy Spirit to the individual soul, and the causal order in which salvation is effected, are also reliant on Platonic and Stoic concepts. For the most part, the Protestant Scholastics followed the Augustinian-Thomist interpretation of the relation of the Spirit to the Father and Son. The *filioque* was not a point of contention with the Roman Catholics, and so was usually simply affirmed without a great deal of argumentation. The most readily available English-language resources for engaging the scholastics are the compendia of Lutheran sources by Heinrich Schmid (1899) and of Reformed sources by Heinrich Heppe (1950).

Because of the characteristic emphasis on the doctrine of justification by faith, most of the Protestant scholastics were more interested in the work than they were in the nature of the Holy Spirit. Treatments of the deity of the Spirit typically involved demonstrations of the way in which Scripture predicated divine attributes (or names or works) to the Spirit. The two most important functions of the Spirit, in the scholastics' view, were the inspiration of the canon of the Bible (not including the Apocrypha, for Protestants) and the sanctification of individual souls. Many of their debates focused on the relation between the human will and the Holy Spirit who, as we have seen, was often associated closely with the divine will in the Western tradition. Some Lutheran scholastics emphasized that without the gracious act of the Spirit a human being is like a stone, wholly inactive. Others resisted the idea that the Holy Spirit effects conversion by a kind of irresistible force, insisting on the freedom of the human will (cf. Schmid, 1899, pp. 471-80).

We find a similar tension in the Reformed tradition, often referred to as the debate between "Calvinists" and "Arminians," the former supporting the doctrine of predestination, and the latter opposing it. On both sides the Augustinian psychological analogy and the correlation between the Spirit and the divine will are taken for granted. The Calvinist Bartholomew Keckermann (d. 1609), for example, explicates the trinitarian relations in this way: "In an essence in which there is perfect knowledge bending back upon itself, an Image is begotten and a Spirit proceeds on the impulse of the will" (cf. Heppe, 1950, p. 107). However, in many of the seminal writings of the Protestant scholastics, the Holy Spirit is hardly mentioned. In those that do focus on the Spirit, the primary effort goes into clarifying the "efficacy" of the Spirit in the causal ordering of the salvation of elect individuals.

The work of Francis Turretin (1623-1687) illustrates this tendency in Reformed scholasticism. In his *Institutes of Elenctic Theology,* he asks whether efficacious grace operates only by moral suasion, which may be received or rejected, or whether it operates by "an invincible and omnipotent suasion which the will of man cannot resist." He affirms the latter, "against the Romanists and Arminians." The human will cannot help resisting grace from the beginning, but neither can it hinder the work of conversion, for God employs in this work an insuperable efficacy and power, an "invincible force" that implies "infallible success" (1992, vol. 2, pp. 546-48). He distinguishes between justification and sanctification, but both have the same "cause" (the death and blood of Christ). Justification, which is objective, is materially and immediately related to this cause, but sanctification, which is subjective, is related "only efficiently and mediately, inasmuch as it is the external impelling cause by which God is moved to give unto us the Holy Spirit, the author of sanctification" (p. 691).

Turretin also points to the work of the Spirit in inspiring the words of the Bible. He calls Scripture "the emanation from the Father of lights and the Sun of righteousness" (1992, vol. 1, p. 63). In his doctrine of God, he follows the medieval pattern of treating the will and intellect of God before exploring the Trinity. In his brief treatment of pneumatology proper, he defends the deity of the Spirit and repeats the traditional Western understanding of the procession of the Spirit from the Father and the Son (1992, vol. 1, pp. 302-10). As we will see in the following section, Turretin's approach had a significant influence on conservative North American theology as it was mediated through the work of Charles Hodge. This was the approach against which many twentieth-century Protestant theologians, both Lutheran and Reformed, would react as they struggled to articulate a more robust understanding of the transforming presence of the Holy Spirit.

Already in the early modern period, however, many Christians were unhappy with the rationalism of the Scholastic approach, preferring to emphasize the importance of pious experience of the Spirit rather than assent to correct propositions about the Spirit. Although the Lutheran theologian Philipp Spener (1635-1705) is often considered the "father of pietism," the movement really began to flourish later in the eighteenth century. Count Ludwig von Zinzendorf (1700-1760) founded the Moravian Church, one of the earliest and most influential pietist movements. Zinzendorf's reflection on the Holy Spirit and his concern for community formation among the Moravian Brethren at Herrnhut were closely connected. In his view, the Christian community is called to mirror the intimacy of the "family" of the Trinity. He calls Christ "our dear husband," the Father "our dear Father," and the Holy Spirit "our dear Mother." For Zinzendorf, the Spirit's motherly office has to do with her birthing, nourishing, educating, and comforting roles in the lives of believers.

As we will see in our exploration of feminist pneumatology, designating the Spirit as the "feminine" in God is not without its problems. However, Gary Kinkel suggests in his book *Our Dear Mother the Spirit* that Zinzendorf's pneumatological writings were tied to his view of women's equality in the Christian community. At Herrnhut women participated in the leadership of the community and helped direct its mission alongside men. According to Kinkel, this practice was supported by Zinzendorf's understanding of the relations among the persons of the Trinity. "There was absolutely no subordination, no hierarchy, in God. Consequently, no subordination or hierarchy of any sort was to be allowed in the Christian community either" (pp. 223-24). Here we can see the contrast between the scholastic focus on the Spirit's causal efficacy in relation to the human will and intellect, and the Pietists' greater emphasis on the Spirit's nurturing presence within the community.

The two most significant eighteenth-century English-speaking theologians, Jonathan Edwards and John Wesley, were both born in 1703. These theologians also shared an interest in emphasizing the importance of religious affections, although for Wesley this took shape as a retrieval of Arminian themes in contrast to Edwards's staunch defense of Calvinism. Both were also key players in what later came to be known as the "Great Awakening," a series of revivals that deeply impacted several areas within England and New England. Edwards's preaching at the religious revivals in 1734-35 in Northampton, Massachusetts, set the stage for the minister George Whitefield's tour of the colonies in 1739-41, which fanned the flames of renewal. Wesley, meanwhile, had been a colleague of Whitefield's at Oxford in the 1720s. In the mid-1730s he went to the American colonies, and interacted with Moravian missionaries there. After returning to England he had an intense conversion experience in 1738 and spent the rest of his life evangelizing and facilitating the formation of communities. This was the beginning of what would later come to be called the Methodist churches.

Although Jonathan Edwards is usually remembered primarily for his fiery sermons and his defense of classically Reformed themes, in the last few decades scholars have drawn attention to other dimensions of his theology, especially in his posthumously published writings. While Edwards did tend to follow the psychological analogies of his tradition, he spelled this out in ways that emphasized delight and joy. For example, in his *Miscellanies* he argues that God is glorified "within Himself" not only in being manifested to himself in his own perfect idea (that is, in his Son), but also by "enjoying and delighting in Himself, by flowing forth in infinite Love and delight towards Himself, or, in his Holy Spirit" (1994, p. 495). In his "Treatise on Grace," he insists that through the indwelling of the divine Spirit, which is "God the Father's and the Son's infinite love and joy in each other," believers are "actually united" to the Holy Spirit (1971, p. 73).

Edwards remains tied to the language of faculty psychology, which he applies to God, but in "An Essay on the Trinity" he emphasizes the "disposition or temper or affection" of the divine mind. The sum of the divine disposition is love, and this "is the Divine disposition or nature that we are made partakers of, 2 Pet. 1:4, for our partaking or communion with God consists in the communion or partaking of the Holy Ghost" (1971, p. 110). Moreover, Edwards sometimes hints at a much more robust role for the

Spirit in relation to the other persons of the Trinity. In his "Fragment on the Trinity" Edwards says that the Holy Spirit "as it were reigns over the Godhead and governs his heart, and wholly influences both the Father and the Son in all they do."[1]

One of the major themes of John Wesley's theology was sanctification, a doctrine in which the Holy Spirit has traditionally played a central role. The famous "Aldersgate experience" of 1738, wherein his heart was "strangely warmed," was interpreted by Wesley in largely pneumatological terms and throughout his life "Spirit" and "spirituality" — pneumatology and ethics — were intimately related (Outler, 1988; Arnett, 1979). Randy Maddox argues that the Spirit is at the center of Wesley's understanding of the Christian life, and that he "*equated* the Holy Spirit with God's gracious empowering Presence restored through Christ" (1994, p. 119). Wesley's pneumatology emphasizes the personhood of the Spirit more than many other Western approaches, and his understanding of God's restoring grace has much in common with the Eastern concept of uncreated grace. Some scholars have even argued that Wesley is closer to the Cappadocians than to Augustine (Staples, 1986).

Wesley was sometimes labeled as an "enthusiast," like so many others who emphasized the witness of the Spirit as much as the revelation of the Word. Yet today we can see that much of the debate between the "Calvinists" and the "Arminians" was based on late medieval and early modern conceptions of causality and faculty psychology, which seemed to force a choice: either limit the power of the human will or limit the power of the divine will (or Spirit). Wesley represents a hinge figure, partially caught in this philosophical either/or but already expressing himself in ways that engage the relational and dynamic thought forms that would come to dominate much of the nineteenth century.

Modern Liberalism and Fundamentalism

Friedrich Schleiermacher (1768-1834) and Charles Hodge (1797-1878) are considered by many to be the founders of modern liberalism and fundamentalism, respectively. Once again, in the context of an introductory text

---

1. Quoted in Sang Lee, *The Philosophical Theology of Jonathan Edwards* (Princeton: Princeton University Press, 1988), p. 195.

on the Holy Spirit, we are forced to risk oversimplification, and the danger is even greater here since the meaning and use of terms like "liberalism" and "fundamentalism" are constantly disputed. Our purpose here is not to solve such disputes, but rather to outline the general contours of the debates over the Holy Spirit between and within the movements to which these labels are typically applied. Broadly speaking, Schleiermacher (who called himself a "Moravian of a higher order") represents an attempt to bring the concerns of Pietism into dialogue with some of the philosophical shifts of the early nineteenth century, while Hodge represents the attempt to conserve the Reformed Protestant Scholastic approach by defending it against those shifts.

Before outlining their views of the Holy Spirit, therefore, we must briefly describe the shifts in question. Modern liberalism and fundamentalism were, in large part, reactions to the writings of two intellectual giants of this period, Immanuel Kant (1724-1804) and G. W. F. Hegel (1770-1831). Kant argued that human (theoretical) reason cannot know things in themselves (noumena) but can only perceive the appearance of things (phenomena). Knowledge involves the synthesis of such perceptions through the pure concepts of the understanding (or categories), namely, quantity, quality, relation, and modality. For our purposes, the important points here are Kant's limitation of reason and his inclusion of "relation" as one of the basic categories of understanding. For Hegel, the category of "relation" was even more central and determinative for his philosophy. In fact, he used this category to redefine human reason rather than to limit it. In his *Phenomenology of the Spirit* (1977) he argued that human knowing participates in the movement of the Spirit toward Absolute Knowing, in which Spirit knows itself as Spirit. He spells this out explicitly in trinitarian terms in his *Lectures on the Philosophy of Religion* (1987). However, many theologians felt that his stress on the immanence of the Spirit collapsed into pantheism, in contrast to Kant's emphasis on the transcendence and unknowability of God, which reinforced a kind of dualism.

Both philosophers, however, contributed to a major shift away from reliance on the category of "substance," which had dominated all three of the ancient schools of Greek philosophy and guided so much of Christian theological discourse about the Spirit as "immaterial substance." The story of the turn toward privileging relationality over substance, in which earlier philosophers like John Locke and David Hume, and later philosophers like Charles Peirce and Edmund Husserl also played a significant role, is too complicated to rehearse here (cf. Shults, 2003). However, it is too important not to mention. The emphasis on relationality shaped the revival of trinitarian doctrine in the twentieth century, and, as we will see later in this chapter, many of the pneumatological proposals of the last few decades tend to privilege the relations among the persons rather than beginning with the concept of a unitary divine substance. This in turn is connected to the integration of the doctrine of the Spirit with the relational dynamics of holistic spiritual transformation that facilitates attention to the communal and ecological aspects of pneumatology. But before we get too far ahead of ourselves, let us return to Schleiermacher and Hodge, whose views of the Holy Spirit were shaped by their engagement with these philosophical developments.

Friedrich Schleiermacher accepted Kant's limitation of reason, but argued that the theological discipline of dogmatics ought to be concerned not with knowing (or doing), but with the "modification of Feeling, or of immediate self-consciousness," which is expressed in piety. In the Introduction to *The Christian Faith*, he asserts that the common essence of all forms of pious feeling is "the consciousness of being absolutely dependent, or which is the same thing, of being in relation with God" (1989, pp. 5, 12). For Schleiermacher Christian dogmatics is the explication of the contents of the pious human self-consciousness, which he also refers to as God-consciousness, or the feeling of absolute dependence. He rejected Hegel's speculation about the "being" of God, insisting that we should limit our theological assertions to the content of pious self-consciousness. Like Hegel, however, Schleiermacher linked human reason to the divine Spirit, although in a quite different way. Inasmuch as "the [human] reason is completely one with the divine Spirit, the divine Spirit can itself be conceived as the highest enhancement of the human reason, so that the difference between the two is made to disappear . . . If, then, the human reason itself in a sense contains that which is produced by the divine Spirit, the latter does not in this connection, at least, go beyond the former" (p. 65).

Schleiermacher's treatment of the doctrine of the Holy Spirit is closely connected, formally and materially, to his understanding of the fellowship of the Christian church. For example, he writes that "the expression 'Holy Spirit' must be understood to mean the vital unity of the Christian fellowship as a moral personality; and this . . . we might denote by the phrase, its *common spirit*" (1989, p. 535, emphasis in original). In other words, for Schleiermacher we cannot speak of the Spirit apart from pious experience within the community. His first theorem on this topic (§123) is: "The Holy Spirit is the union of the Divine Essence with human nature in the form of the common spirit animating the life in common of believers" (p. 569). Schleiermacher's view of salvation is certainly christocentric, insofar as he focuses on the way in which the Redeemer (Christ) unites believers with him by "assuming" them into the power of his perfect God-consciousness. However, he also makes clear that this experience cannot be separated (or even distinguished) from the indwelling of and partaking in the Spirit. "[B]eing drawn by that union into the fellowship of believers, having a share in the Holy Spirit, and being drawn into living fellowship with Christ — must simply mean one and the same thing" (p. 575).

Schleiermacher does not seem worried that his explication of pious Christian feeling does not have significant biblical warrant; "however much the letter of Scripture may seem to contradict us, the spirit of the New Testament is on our side" (1989, p. 570). This is in accordance with his method, in which the pious self-consciousness is privileged as the primary source for dogmatics. Moreover, he is not interested in providing assurance that his formulations are consistent with traditional expressions of the doctrine of the third person of the Trinity. Debates over such matters as the psychological analogy or the *filioque* clause are relatively unimportant for Schleiermacher, both because of his aversion to speculation about the "being" of God and because of his desire to discover the common element in pious self-consciousness among all Christians, including the first disciples. We can discover this commonality "if need be without a doctrine of the Holy Spirit, just as the disciples understood their own condition without any such doctrine" (p. 490). Schleiermacher places his treatment of the Trinity at the end of *The Christian Faith,* noting that the orthodox formulation of the doctrine is not "an immediate or even a necessary combination of utterances concerning the Christian self-consciousness" (p. 740). The original tendency of the doctrine, he argues, was to insist that God is somehow present in "our consciousness of Christ" and in the "common Spirit of the Church," but dogmatics is not required to (indeed should not) engage in speculation about the "being of God in Himself" (pp. 747-48).

Throughout the nineteenth century (and continuing to the present) theologians associated with the modern "liberal" Protestant tradition have been heavily indebted to Schleiermacher in their interpretations of the transforming experience of the Holy Spirit. Such theologians have typically emphasized that salvation has to do not only with the illumination of individuals but with the formation of communities, often leading to a focus primarily on ethics rather than belief. Theologians in this tradition have also generally followed Schleiermacher in downplaying the importance of traditional language about the Trinity, agreeing with him that much of that discourse inappropriately attempts to speculate about the being (substance) of God rather than attending to God's active relation to humankind in history. Finally, the divine Spirit is commonly described in ways that point to the presence of God in and to all of creation, not just human beings. All of these tendencies can be found in major "liberal" theologians in the twentieth century, such as Paul Tillich (1963) and Geoffrey Lampe (1977).

Charles Hodge's defense of many traditional formulations of the doctrine of the Holy Spirit, and his theological method in general, was explicitly shaped by his suspicion of Kantian and Hegelian tendencies in late nineteenth-century philosophy, and by his antagonism toward Schleiermacher in particular. Early in his three-volume *Systematic Theology,* he names Schleiermacher as the "most distinguished and influential advocate" of the "mystical" method in theology, which he takes as denying the possibility of "supernatural objective presentation or communication of truth to the mind, by the Spirit of God" (1981, vol. 1, pp. 8-9). For his part, Hodge follows what he calls the "inductive" method, in which the theologian collects facts from the Bible and deduces principles from them. He acknowledges, with Augustine and Calvin, the role of the "inward teaching of the Spirit," but this is "confined to truths objectively revealed in the Scriptures" (vol. 1, p. 15). On the one hand, Hodge believes that this method protects against the "speculative" tendencies of German idealism (especially Hegel). On the other hand, it supports his contention (against Kant) that human reason can and does know the being of God. In fact, Hodge insists, "We know God in the same sense in which we know ourselves and things out of ourselves" (vol. 1, p. 365).

Hodge's arrangement of the topics of Christian doctrine is strongly reminiscent of Francis Turretin, whose *Institutes* he used as the basis for his classes at Princeton Theological Seminary. He begins with an extensive prolegomenon explaining the role of reason in theology and positing the inspiration of Scripture, which provides the foundation for knowledge of God. Part I is "Theology Proper," in which the "theistic" idea of God is defended and proved, followed by an exposition of the divine nature and attributes, including the intellect and will of God. After the "nature" of God has been explained, he turns to the doctrine of the Trinity. Acknowledging the "mysterious" character of the traditional formulations of the one substance and the three persons, Hodge nevertheless defends the basic Augustinian approach, including the psychological analogy and the *filioque*. It is important to note that in their systematic presentations of doctrine both Schleiermacher and Hodge follow the typical Western ordering, initiated by Thomas Aquinas, in which the unity of God is treated first and shown to be rational, followed later by an examination of the Trinity, which is taken as somewhat more problematic. This formal decision clearly has some bearing on their valuation and material understanding of the doctrine of the Holy Spirit, which does not play a generative role in their theological systems.

In the conclusion of his short chapter on the Holy Spirit, Hodge compares Schleiermacher's view with the heresies of the Socinians, Arians, and Sabellians, all of whom regarded the Holy Spirit merely as the power of God, the "manifested divine efficiency." He notes that for Schleiermacher God is "only the unity of the causality" that is manifested in the world, although he calls that causality viewed in Christ "Son" and that causality viewed in the church "Spirit." For his part, Hodge defends the Nicene-Constantinopolitan Creed, in relation to which he argues "there has been no diversity of faith on this subject among those recognized as Christians" (1981, vol. 1, p. 534). Later in Part III (Soteriology), Hodge treats the Holy Spirit in relation to the sanctification of the soul, which occurs after vocation, regeneration, faith, and justification in the order of salvation. There he emphasizes the "inward work" of the Spirit, which has to do not with "feeling," but with the "enlightenment of the mind," through which "the soul is thus raised above the world" (vol. 3, pp. 229-30).

Hodge's influence was enormous, framing North American theological debate in terms of the Reformed Protestant scholastic tradition which he had mediated. The "fundamentalist" movement in the early twentieth century found inspiration in Hodge as they struggled against the materialist philosophy they perceived as driving the Darwinian theory of evolution, and the secularist accommodation they identified in modern liberal theology. There is no reference to the Holy Spirit in the statement of the five "fundamentals" that the 1910 General Assembly of the Presbyterian Church sought to conserve. After the Fundamentalist-Modernist conflict split the denomination, theologians who aligned themselves with "Old

Princeton" would continue to treat the Holy Spirit primarily in relation to the inspiration of the Bible and the sanctification of the individual soul. Meanwhile, led by Billy Graham and others, the "evangelical" movement explicitly attempted to find a middle ground between these two subcultures within North American Protestant Christianity. Most theologians associated with this form of "evangelicalism" would continue (and still continue) to subordinate pneumatology to christology, both formally and materially. Within the last few years, however, this stream of the tradition has begun to concentrate some of its scholarly effort more explicitly on the Holy Spirit (e.g., Pinnock, 1996).

The movement that would eventually inspire the academic revival of pneumatology, to which we referred in the Introduction, was largely ignored (or suppressed) by both liberals and fundamentalists when it exploded into existence around the turn of the twentieth century. The enthusiastic reception of the Spirit that characterized this movement would be greeted with suspicion across denominations, but its phenomenal growth and pervasive global influence would lead more and more theologians of all types to pay fresh attention to the significance of the Holy Spirit in Christian theology and practice.

Pentecostalism

Historians of Pentecostalism are increasingly pointing to the simultaneous eruption of charismatic renewal worldwide during the first decade of the twentieth century (cf. Anderson, 2004). However, two developments in the United States are typically connected to the emergence of the movement: one associated with the work of Charles F. Parham and his students in Topeka, Kansas, and another with the revival that took place between 1906 and 1909 under the leadership of African American Holiness preacher William J. Seymour in a church on Azusa Street in Los Angeles, California. The latter is certainly the better known. Almost every day thousands of men and women from diverse social and racial backgrounds packed into this Los Angeles church to immerse themselves in the transforming presence of the Spirit. There were testimonies of healing, exorcism, and glossolalia ("speaking in tongues"), as in the days following the outpouring of the Spirit at Pentecost reported in Acts 2.

While scholars debate the precise time and place of the origin of

Pentecostalism, no one disputes its astonishing growth and global impact on twentieth-century Christianity. "Classical" Pentecostalism is the term commonly used to refer to churches and movements that grew out of and explicitly embraced the extraordinary experiences of the Spirit that characterized the Azusa Street revival. In the 1950s and 1960s groups within several mainline Protestant denominations as well as the Roman Catholic Church also began to report manifestations and gifts (*charismata*) of the Spirit, although not always with the same intensity. These developments, which also led to the formation of a variety of "nondenominational" churches in the 1970s and beyond, are sometimes referred to as the "charismatic renewal." Across the globe Christian communities have emerged that place special emphasis on the experience of the gifts of the Spirit; these are sometimes called "neocharismatics." If one includes all of these groups, the Pentecostal movement now claims over 500 million adherents, the majority of whom live in the Southern and Eastern Hemispheres. If current growth trends continue, it is estimated that by 2025 the number may reach 800 million (cf. Burgess and van der Maas, 2002).

In this context we will use the term "Pentecostal" to refer to this diverse set of Christian religious groups that enthusiastically attend to the gifts and manifestations of the Spirit in their spiritual practices. Early interpretations of this transforming experience focused on "Spirit baptism." Of course, questions arose from the beginning: How does "being filled with the Holy Spirit" relate to "accepting Jesus as Savior"? Is Spirit baptism necessary for salvation, and is it always connected with experiences such as glossolalia? Although Pentecostals debated such questions, they shared an emphasis on the value and importance of Spirit baptism for Christian life. Being "filled" with the Spirit usually occurred after "conversion," and most often through prayer and the "laying on of hands." In his *Introduction to Pentecostalism*, Allan Anderson depicts Spirit baptism among Azusa Street worshipers as first involving a "longing for the experience, followed by extreme physical sensations and feelings of elation . . . culminating in a release usually involving speaking in tongues, either at the same time as the 'baptism' or soon afterwards" (2004, p. 188). Many contemporary Pentecostals experience Spirit baptism in much the same way.

Spirit baptism and the use of the *charismata* are intimately tied to the worship and formation of the Christian community. Pentecostals believe that being filled with the Spirit empowers them to live holy lives, to become effective witnesses, and to use the gifts for the edification of the body of Christ (cf. Anderson, 2004, p. 231). The manifestations of this experience are often ecstatic and vocal. In her *Saints in Exile*, womanist theologian and ethicist Cheryl J. Sanders notes that in the "sanctified church" (that is, the black Holiness-Pentecostal tradition), spontaneous shouts of praise such as "hallelujah," "amen," "yes," "praise the Lord," and "thank you, Jesus" are characteristic elements of the shared experience of the Spirit (1996, p. 61). Other scholars have argued that the ecstatic experiences of the Spirit in Pentecostalism are connected to the movement's roots in the religion of the African Diaspora, which integrated aspects of African religion with Western Christianity in the experience of slavery (cf. MacRobert, 1997; Sanders, 1996).

In corporate Pentecostal worship services of all types, participants often experience a sense of rapture and joy, which overflows in a variety of physical expressions including speaking in tongues, prophesying, healing, testifying, shouting, weeping, laughing, waving flags, clapping, raising hands, falling, and dancing. Daniel Albrecht describes Pentecostal spirituality as holistic. "Pentecostals seek to worship their God with their whole being. They have intuitively presented their bodies, their physicality, as instruments of worship. They seek to move with the Spirit, but not as incorporeal selves. Pentecostals experience God as embodied people, propelled by the Spirit and by their songs" (1999, p. 247).

For the first few decades of the movement, many Pentecostals were suspicious of both secular and established Christian universities and colleges, founding their own schools or Bible institutes. In the latter part of the twentieth century, however, a growing number of Pentecostal scholars have not only joined but thrived within the broader theological academy. This has both strengthened Pentecostal scholarship and inspired non-Pentecostal theologians to pay more attention to the doctrine and experience of the Holy Spirit. Because the Pentecostal renewal transgressed not only Protestant denominational boundaries but spilled into (and out of) the Roman Catholic and Eastern Orthodox traditions, it has uniquely contributed to the ecumenical dialogue, a phenomenon we will explore in more detail below. Veli-Matti Kärkkäinen's *Pneumatology: The Holy Spirit in Ecumenical, International, and Contextual Perspective* (2002) provides an introduction to and example of this linking of the growth of charismatic spirituality to ecumenism (and other twentieth-century developments).

Kärkkäinen also illustrates two other ways in which Pentecostal theologians are contributing to the broader dialogue, emphasizing the role that pneumatology can and ought to play in the formulation of the doctrine of the Trinity and in the dialogue among religions. It might seem that these latter two goals are mutually exclusive, since interreligious dialogue often remains at the level of generic ideas regarding an ultimate reality while the Trinity is a belief peculiar to the Christian religion. Nevertheless, in an essay on "How to Speak of the Spirit among Religions," Kärkkäinen argues that "the proper context for advancing a pneumatological theology of religions is a healthy trinitarian framework" (2006, p. 48). The concept of the Spirit can be articulated as a principle of relationality in which we understand trinitarian communion as providing room for both genuine diversity and unity, which allows and even promotes an interdependent relational encounter with the religious "Other."

The possibilities for a pneumatological approach to ecumenical and interreligious dialogue have been explored in more detail by Pentecostal theologian Amos Yong. In his *Beyond the Impasse: Toward a Pneumatological Theology of Religions* (2002), he emphasizes the universal presence and activity of God's Spirit in all human life. Engaging a variety of Christian traditions, including Eastern Orthodoxy and evangelicalism, Yong develops a "foundational pneumatology" that is open to discerning the work of the divine Spirit in all the religions of the world. In his more recent *The Spirit Poured Out on All Flesh* (2005), Yong weaves together soteriological, ecclesiological, Trinitarian, and eschatological themes, suggesting that Pentecostal interpretations of the transforming experience of the Spirit can contribute to new possibilities for improved relations amidst genuine *differences*. In his final chapter, Yong explores the implications of a pneumatological approach to a theology of creation, suggesting that attention to the presence of the Spirit throughout all of the cosmos might provide new opportunities for the dialogue between theology and contemporary science (cf. Yong, 2006; Macchia, 2006).

Yong recognizes that his proposal to *start* with pneumatology will feel threatening to many theologians who might worry that this unhinges Spirit from Word, or that it could sponsor "enthusiastic" individual interpretations of the Bible untethered to the long tradition of the Christian church. In his *Spirit-Word-Community: Theological Hermeneutics in Trinitarian Perspective,* Yong argues for a "trialectic" model of theological interpretation in which "Spirit and Word mutually interpenetrate and coinhere in Community without losing their distinctness" (2002, p. 18). Nevertheless, following the lead of Henry Pitt van Dusen (1958), he *begins* with the Spirit for rhetorical, programmatic, and theological reasons, insisting that only in this way can Western theology overcome its habit of subordinating the Spirit to the Word, which registers its effect in the *filioque* as well as in other doctrines. Yong sets out and defends a "trinitarian metaphysics that is relational, realistic and communal" (p. 25), in which he privileges the categories of relationality, rationality, and dynamic life in the Spirit.

Although North American conservative theologians, both fundamentalists and evangelicals, have much in common with Pentecostal theologians, the former are often nervous about the way in which the latter connect the Spirit to the community and to the cosmos, as well as their openness to dialogue with other religions, all of which reminds them of modern liberalism. Yet these are not the only voices that are shaping the academic revival of interest in the Spirit, which continues to spread across denominations. In the next three parts of this chapter, we will outline other twentieth-century theological developments that have contributed to and shaped this new academic interest in pneumatology.

The Ecumenical Movement

The World Council of Churches (WCC) was founded in 1948 in order to promote ecumenical dialogue, that is, conversation across Christian denominations and traditions. As Kärkkäinen (2002, pp. 98-104) points out, for many years the doctrine of the Holy Spirit has been a prominent theme at the conferences of the WCC. Indeed, at its seventh General Assembly in 1991 in Canberrra, Australia, the WCC focused explicitly on pneumatology. This is partly due to the increase in Pentecostal and charismatic participants, a number which has grown rapidly since the 1960s. Yet even apart from that, given that the organization's explicit mission is to encourage worldwide Christian unity, it makes sense that the WCC would pay special attention to one of the issues that was a key factor in some of the major splits in Christendom. Employing the theme "Come, Holy Spirit — Renew the Whole Creation," the Assembly explored pneumatological resources for facilitating reconciliation and dialogue among churches, cultures, and other religions.

As we saw above, the addition of the *filioque* to the creed in the fifth century was one of the factors that contributed to the mutual condemnations of the Western (Roman Catholic) and Eastern (Orthodox) Churches. For this reason, much of the ecumenical dialogue at this level has focused on this issue, the resolution of which many see as the most promising way toward the restoration of full communion between — or even reunion of — these traditions. The last half-century has witnessed an unprecedented willingness on both sides to explore new ways to clarify and articulate the Spirit's relation to the Father and the Son. The fruit of such dialogue can be found in several collections of essays that compare, contrast, critique, and reconstruct Eastern and Western approaches to the doctrine of the Spirit and the Trinity (cf. Küng, 1979; Vischer, 1981; Schwöbel, 1995; and Davis, Kendall, and O'Collins, 1999). In this section we will outline the proposals of a few of the major representatives of the traditions most heavily involved in ecumenical dialogue about the *filioque.*

The ecumenical openness expressed in the Second Vatican Council of the Roman Catholic Church, which was held from 1962 until 1965, along with the charismatic movement that swept through the churches worldwide in the 1950s and 1960s, created an environment in which theologians found new encouragement for exploring the doctrine of the Holy Spirit. The most well-known contribution to this literature is the three-volume work *I Believe in the Holy Spirit* by Yves Congar, who was a participant in the dialogues surrounding Vatican II. Congar traces the biblical and historical development of the Christian understanding of the experience of the Spirit. Here we are dealing not only with a topic that may help facilitate communion among churches, but with the divine "principle of communion" already at work in the church and world. The presence of the Spirit strengthens God's people, establishing them in oneness, holiness, catholicity, and apostolicity. Congar affirms the extraordinary charisms of the renewal movement as a manifestation of the communion-bringing Spirit's manifold gifting of individuals and institutions. His own constructive proposal regarding the *filioque* calls for concessions on both sides: the Roman Catholic Church could remove the term from the creed for the sake of ecumenical humility and solidarity, but on the condition that the Orthodox Church acknowledge that the term may be interpreted in a nonheretical way (1997, vol. 2, p. 214).

There is still much ecumenical work to do in the healing of the rift caused by the *filioque* controversy, but significant strides have been made in recent years. In the *New Catechism of the Catholic Church,* first published under the authority of Pope John Paul II in 1992, the Eastern view of the

Spirit's procession is described as having a "legitimate complementarity" with the Western view. The Eastern position (if understood non-rigidly) in no way affects "the identity of faith in the reality of the same mystery confessed."[2] Another symbolic gesture of apparent openness can be observed in the publication of *Dominus Iesus* ("Lord Jesus") on September 5, 2000. This document was composed by Cardinal Joseph Ratzinger when he was prefect of the Congregation for the Doctrine of the Faith, before he became Pope Benedict XVI in 2005. In its opening article, it repeats the text of the Nicene-Constantinopolitan Creed *without* the *filioque* clause; "and the Son" is simply left out without any comment. Many, however, are concerned that the remainder of the document, with its emphasis on the unicity and necessity of the church led by the successor of Peter, takes away any possibility for authentic ecumenical dialogue.

We do not have the space in this introductory text to point to all the ecumenical efforts among Protestant denominations and between various Protestant traditions, Roman Catholicism, and Eastern Orthodoxy. Yet one dialogue worth highlighting is that between the Reformed and Orthodox traditions; as part of this conversation the Reformed Scottish theologian Tom Smail suggests that the formula "*from* the Father *through* the Son" might win acceptance on both sides if it is understood in a way that "takes full account of the Eastern emphasis on the priority of the Father as the source of the Spirit in a way that the present *filioque* clause does not" and that makes clear, "as Western teaching requires, that the ministry and the person of the Spirit are in the closest possible relation to the ministry and person of the Son" (2002, pp. 138-39). In relation to Roman Catholicism, similar opportunities have emerged. For example, the Roman Catholic theologian Alexandre Ganoczy has suggested that the pneumatological achievements of Vatican II actually open up new possibilities for a theological integration of concerns shared by both the theologians of Trent and John Calvin, indicating that the French Reformer may be regarded as a representative of a "substantial Catholicity" (1979, p. 53).

One of the most active participants in ecumenical dialogue from the Eastern Orthodox tradition has been the theologian John Zizioulas. Zizioulas has been particularly attentive to the differences between the way in which the traditional Eastern and Western positions utilize the concepts of person and causality in the doctrine of the Trinity, which in turn rami-

---

2. *Catechism of the Catholic Church* (Chicago: Loyola University Press, 1994), p. 248.

fies into pneumatology. In *Being as Communion* (1985), he argues that for the Cappadocians and most other Eastern theologians the category of "person" is not a subset of the category of "substance" as it sometimes appears in Western definitions. For the Greek Fathers, the ontological "principle" or "cause" of the being and life of God "does not consist in the one substance of God but in the *hypostasis,* that is, *the person of the Father.* The one God is not the one substance but the Father, who is the 'cause' both of the generation of the Son and of the procession of the Spirit." The monarchy of the Father privileges personhood, rather than substance, as the ground of all being as communion. "Outside the Trinity there is no God, that is, no divine substance, because the ontological 'principle' of God is the Father. The personal existence of God (the Father) constitutes His substance, makes it hypostases. The being of God is identified with the person" (1985, pp. 40-41).

Zizioulas has also argued that part of the problem in the *filioque* debates is the Western reliance on the philosophical category of "substance" as the primary way to make sense of the relations among the persons of the Trinity. In a chapter on "Pneumatology and the Importance of the Person" he explores the way in which the concept of "substance" (and so *homoousion*) functioned in the second ecumenical council, that of Constantinople. He contends that the main point of the council's use of the term "substance" was to underscore the distinction between created and uncreated being as the basis for clarifying the way in which the (uncreated) Holy Spirit — as giver of life — makes possible the communion of the created with the uncreated divine nature (2006, p. 183). "Substance" was not used, argues Zizioulas, as the basic category for speaking of the divine nature or the relations among the divine persons, as it was in many later Western formulations. The real issue behind the *filioque,* he insists, "concerns the question whether the ultimate ontological category in theology is the person or substance" (p. 196). Acknowledging the work of Congar and others on this topic, Zizioulas calls the *filioque* an "open question," one which might be resolved by "a deeper theological re-reception of Constantinople" (p. 199).

One of the reasons Eastern Orthodoxy has resisted the *filioque,* argues Zizioulas, is that it appears to privilege christology over pneumatology by reinforcing the notion that the work of Christ is "objective" while the work of the Spirit is only "subjective," the latter extending or applying the former. This in turn can lead to an ecclesiology in which the church exists already "in Christ," to which the Spirit comes later for the sake of gifting or equipping. Zizioulas argues that "pneumatology must be made *constitutive* of Christology and ecclesiology, i.e., condition the very being of Christ and the Church" (1985, p. 139). While Christ "in-stitutes" the church, the Spirit "con-stitutes" the church by transforming its members into the corporate personality of Christ, that is, by making the "one" into the "many" through loving, self-giving communal relations. The church is not self-sufficient, based on its having been founded in the past, but "has its roots in the future and its branches in the present" (p. 59). The church exists "epicletically," constantly dependent on the arrival of the Holy Spirit. *Epiclesis* refers to the invocation of the Spirit, which is a central part of the liturgy of the Eucharist in Eastern Orthodox churches, in distinction from many Western liturgies that focus more exclusively on *anamnesis*, the remembrance of the work of the Son. Zizioulas describes the Holy Spirit as confronting "the process of history with its consummation, with its transformation and transfiguration. By bringing the eschata into history, [the Spirit] does not vivify a pre-existing structure; He *creates* one; He changes linear historicity into a *presence*" (p. 180).

Russian Orthodox theologian Vladimir Lossky describes the way in which Eastern theology has upheld the importance of the "economy of the Spirit" as well as the "economy of the Son," refusing to subordinate the former to the latter, a tendency he finds encapsulated in many Western interpretations of the *filioque*. For the mystical theology of the Eastern church, he argues, Pentecost is the object and final goal of the divine economy. The deification of creatures through the Spirit is inseparable from the incarnation of the Son, and vice versa (1998, pp. 159, 170). André de Halleux offers this summary of Lossky's understanding of the spiritual and ecclesial implications of the Western subordination of the Spirit to the economy of the Word:

> The goal of the Christian way of life therefore becomes the *imitatio Christi*, no longer a deification by the Holy Spirit . . . The people of God are subjected to the body of Christ, the charism is made subordinate to the institution, inner freedom to imposed authority, prophetism to juridicism, mysticism to scholasticism, the laity to the clergy, the universal priesthood to the ministerial hierarchy, and finally the college of bishops to the primacy of the Pope. (Quoted in Congar, 1997, vol. 3, p. 208)

Throughout this book we have tried to identify the reciprocal interaction between interpretations of the doctrine of the Holy Spirit and experiences of spiritual transformation in community. In previous sections we have already seen how this works in the tension between charism and institution, as well as mysticism and scholasticism. Even as they address issues that are deeply important to ecumenical dialogue about the Spirit, Lossky's insights point to another tension: the one between the prophetic and the juridical, i.e., between voices of reform and voices upholding the legal status quo. It is to this tension that we now turn our attention.

Feminist and Liberation Theology

Another factor in the revival of pneumatological doctrine in the twentieth century was the chorus of theologians who began to speak up in the midst of and on behalf of the poor and oppressed. Although the movements generally referred to as feminist and liberation theology are distinct in many ways, and each composed of quite diverse approaches, it is nevertheless possible to point to some concerns and philosophical tendencies shared by many of their participants. Both movements are constituted by their concern for the oppressed, whether that oppression is based primarily on gender, race, or class. Many theologians have taken up the concerns of those who are oppressed based on more than one of these factors (e.g., mujerista and womanist theology, which are concerned with the perspectives of Hispanic and African American women respectively). On the whole, feminist and liberation theology, both of which emerged within the Western tradition, have not paid as much attention to pneumatology as they have to other theological themes, such as christology or soteriology.

When they have focused on the doctrine of the Holy Spirit, however, many of the proposals of such theologians have more or less explicitly been shaped by their reactions to traditional formulations of the doctrine of the Spirit that rely on medieval or early modern concepts of matter, person, and force. In this section, we will pay special attention to the way in which some of the contributors to these movements have responded to and participated in ways of interpreting the transforming experience of the Spirit in relation to *embodied action, egalitarian community,* and *emancipating power.*

It is easy to understand why feminist theologians have been resistant to the denigration of matter and embodiment so pervasive in traditional Christian theology. The privileging of "immaterial" intellectuality over "material" physicality, and the association of these concepts with masculinity and femininity respectively, has helped to authorize the devaluation of women and of embodiment in spiritual practice. Many feminist theologians have argued that embodiment is in fact integral to what it means to be a whole person liberated by and living in the Spirit. In her *Sensing the Spirit: The Holy Spirit in Feminist Perspective* (1999), Rebecca Button Prichard weaves together a variety of biblical, historical, autobiographical, and theological perspectives, arguing against a "ghostly" and for a "tangible" understanding of the experience of the Spirit.

Embodiment is not just about human bodies, but the whole of "material" creation, which has led many feminist theologians to link pneumatology to ecological concerns. For example, in her *Life Abundant* (2001), Sallie McFague describes "life in the Spirit" as a "cruciform" way of living that is frugal, restrained, and communal — always oriented toward empowering the poor and sustaining the planet in practical ways. In her *Women, Earth, and Creator Spirit* (1993), Elizabeth A. Johnson contends that the marginalization of women and the exploitation of the earth are closely related, and that when concrete existence is downplayed or diminished, it becomes too easy to ignore the ethical and political demands of Christian life — namely, resisting women's subjugation and the earth's degradation. She also explicitly links her understanding of the Spirit to a call to spiritual conversion. Learning to care for each other and the earth will require us to "assume our responsibility as co-partners with the Creator Spirit" (p. 63). Elsewhere she writes of the Creator Spirit as "the matrix of the world's dynamic existence. . . . The primal ground, sustaining power, and ultimate destiny of the whole universe" (2005a, p. 207). Johnson seeks to dismantle the dualism between matter and spirit that reinforces the tendency to separate the ethical and political dimensions of embodied Christian practice from the intellectual dimensions of life with and in the Spirit of God.

Here we can see the connection between the emphasis on embodied action and the concern for egalitarian communion. Feminist theology tends to challenge both the ideal of the autonomous individual and the hierarchical structuring of societies that promote the advancement of their power over others, stressing instead the importance of dynamic reciprocity and mutual interdependence for healthy community. Elizabeth Johnson illustrates this theme as well in her pneumatological reflections in *She Who Is* ([1992] 2005). Johnson observes that Christian theology has often associated the Spirit with femininity, and at the same time has consistently subjugated or downplayed the role of the Holy Spirit among the personal relations within the Trinity. Drawing on the Wisdom/*Sophia* tradition, she offers an alternative to more hierarchical constructions of the doctrine of God by re-envisioning the Trinity as an equal community of divine persons constituted by reciprocal relations. Johnson speaks of Spirit-*Sophia* as the Wisdom of God who, in communion with Jesus-*Sophia* and Mother-*Sophia*, creates, renews, empowers, and graces all things.

Catherine LaCugna has also emphasized the importance of conceptualizing the Trinity as equal persons in communion. In *God for Us* (1992), she especially decries ways in which God has been depicted as a "self-sufficient masculine Father-God" whose power resides in his ability to have power over others. LaCugna argues that the "strongest possible defense against sexism is indeed to argue ontologically . . . that the *being* of God is utterly antithetical to every kind of subordination and subservience" (p. 287). We should think of the divine *arché* not as a dominant self-sufficient individual substance, but as the personal life of the "fecund, ecstatic God who is matrix of all" (p. 398). We can also point to the work of Nancy Victorin-Vangerud, who draws on a wide array of sociological, psychological, philosophical, and theological sources in order to construct a "feminist maternal pneumatology of mutual recognition" that highlights the dynamics of the self-other relation. Using family as her primary metaphor, she challenges what she calls "poisonous pneumatologies" — those that mirror patriarchal models of family that emphasize the will of the authoritative One over the mutuality of the Many. Alternatively, she outlines a doctrine of the Spirit that begins with intersubjectivity and mutuality, and advocates a trinitarian pneumatology that "displaces the Father's consuming ego . . . with the Spirit's erotic We of the whole creation" (2000, p. 210).

Liberating empowerment is a third prominent theme in feminist discourse on the Spirit. For example, Brazilian feminist theologian Ivone Gebara describes God's Spirit as the source that fills women with power to press toward freedom. For her, the Spirit is "breath of life, energy refusing to be locked in a box"; further, this infinite divine energy fills and indwells women, empowering them to struggle against evil: "The power called freedom for many women is like being pregnant with the Spirit" (1996, p. 147).

In her *Saints in Exile* (1996), womanist Pentecostal theologian Cheryl J. Sanders discusses the empowering effects of following the Spirit's lead in the context of African American Holiness Pentecostal worship services. To shout "Yes, Lord!" in the Holiness Pentecostal congregation is to surrender to the Holy Spirit's summons, and thus to receive power for holy living (p. 68). For many feminist theologians life in the Spirit brings empowerment through hope for a new future of freedom. More than wishful thinking, however, the Spirit grants prophetic boldness to women as they orient themselves against oppressive structures and welcome new forms of life together that anticipate the eschatological healing of the nations and the cosmos. Here the Spirit is not understood as a "will" that pushes inexorably from the past, but as an evocative personal presence that calls creatures toward and into a future of fellowship within divine life.

Like feminist theology, liberation theology is also characterized by a commitment to standing in solidarity with the oppressed, but most of the theologians associated with this movement have focused on the experiences of the poor, especially in Central and South America. Convinced that a "preferential option for the poor" is at the core of Christianity, such theologians expose and challenge misuses of power by speaking out against structures of institutionalized oppression (such as globalization, neocolonialism, or consumerism), and holding the church accountable for the ways that it has been (and continues to be) complicit with dynamics of injustice. The concrete political and economic freedom of all people is an explicit goal, and is often connected to the arrival of the reign of God. The pneumatological writings of liberationists are diverse and multilayered, but we can pick out the same three broad themes: embodied action, egalitarian community, and emancipating power. Although these themes are dominant among many influential liberation theologians (e.g., Sobrino, 1988), we will point briefly to the way in which they are woven into the work of two in particular, José Comblin and Leonardo Boff.

As Comblin observes in *The Holy Spirit and Liberation* (1989), part of the process of liberation for the poor is coming to understand themselves as agents, as persons capable of action that will shape the future. This involves discovering one's voice and embracing the responsibility to speak. For Comblin, this is irreducibly pneumatological: "The experience of the Spirit is in taking up speech" (p. 27). This liberating and liberated speech is radically embodied and communal. Rejecting common individualistic notions of freedom, he insists that "being free does not mean acting on one's own . . . being free means collaborating in a community" (p. 64). The Spirit brings freedom, community, and life, but the "first aim" of the Spirit is bringing new forms of "*bodily* life." Human bodily life is personal, and lived at various levels of intensity; the Spirit gives fresh impulse to this bodily life and the body produces effects through the energizing of the Spirit, which is carrying the whole of creation toward final resurrection and transformation (pp. 73-75). The Spirit is the divine agent of transformation who acts in history, the "hand" of God (after Irenaeus) that acts from within communities to release people from repressive power structures. Comblin emphasizes that the giving, loving, and living Spirit grants freedom to God's people so that they are able to find fellowship and solidarity with one another as they work together for justice.

In his *Church: Charism and Power* (1985), Leonardo Boff challenges the traditional correlation between the Spirit and the power of the institutional church. He argues that power should be located in grassroots Christian groups (ecclesial base communities), not only in the hands of the popes, bishops, and decrees of the hierarchical Roman Catholic Church — an institution which, in his words, "no longer exudes happiness or joy, only respectability and weight" (p. 154). The traditional form of ecclesial power has been "power-over"; Boff calls for a model of "power-with(in)" the Spirit of God, who calls each member of the community to use his or her gifts (charisms) to love, serve, and lead in the community. "The Church is alive where the Spirit is not suffocated. Diverse *charisms* abound, creativity flourishes, and Jesus' message becomes, again, good news" (p. 158). Like many feminist theologians, Boff maintains that the way in which we understand the Trinity has direct social implications. In *Holy Trinity, Perfect Community* (1988) he rejects the notion of God as a single ruling monarch, and resists any subordination in the Trinity. The pattern for the liberation of human existence is found in the Trinity; the difference and distinction, equality and perfect communion of Father, Son, and Spirit is the ground and goal of perfect human community. For Boff the Holy Spirit is the "liberating principle" who, in perfect union with Father and Son, brings freedom from social oppressions by stirring people to acts of love and justice together, which draws them into the dynamism of God's life.

For most liberation and feminist theologians, authentic life in the Spirit, or true spirituality, is marked by embodied action — the performance of loving and just deeds that improve the everyday experiences of the poor and oppressed. These actions may include such things as building schools or churches, vocally protesting governmental corruption, or advocating literacy, all of which participate in the formation of more egalitarian forms of community. We can understand why such theologians are more enthusiastic about a future in which the Spirit transforms current power structures that liberate the oppressed from their bondage within the status quo. These movements, like the rapid spread of Pentecostalism worldwide, have contributed significantly to the academic revival of interest in the Holy Spirit. Yet white male theologians solidly established within mainline institutions have also have contributed to this revival, even when not explictly engaged in ecumenical discourse.

Other Twentieth-Century Reconstructions

We begin with Karl Barth, whom many consider to be the most influential Protestant theologian of the twentieth century. Although this Reformed theologian's pneumatology has often been criticized as inadequate, especially in comparison to his more carefully developed christology, in his later writings he increasingly emphasized the importance of the Spirit as a mediating principle in theological formulations (cf. Rosato, 1981). The fifth volume to his *Church Dogmatics*, which would have treated "The Doctrine of Redemption" and focused on pneumatology more explicitly, was never begun. However, already in the fourth volume, "The Doctrine of Reconciliation," Barth had dealt with the Spirit in relation to the church and to Christian life: the gathering, upbuilding, and sending of the community through faith, love, and hope.

Barth's material formulations in pneumatology were less influential than his formal arrangement of themes in the first volume of the *Dogmatics*. In that context, he describes the trinitarian God as having three "modes" of being, derived from the concept of revelation: God is "the One who Reveals Himself," that is, revealer, revelation, and a being revealed (1936, I.1; p. 363). This refiguring of the Augustinian analogy has been much criticized, but Barth's contribution to the revival of interest in the doctrine of the Holy Spirit does not lie here. It lies, rather, in the fact that in reaction to the tendencies of the entire Reformed tradition (from Turretin through Schleiermacher and Hodge and their followers), after his analysis of the nature of dogmatics in relation to the Word of God, Barth treats the doctrine of the Trinity as the *first* material theme. This shift inspired a whole generation of theologians to begin not with generic ideas of the divine nature, but with the concrete act of God in Christ through the Spirit. This helped to promote reflection on the Trinity, which in turn opened conceptual space for more relational and dynamic interpretations of the transforming experience of the Spirit.

Like Barth, Karl Rahner is not known for his pneumatology. However, he too had an enormous effect on the flourishing of reflection on the doctrine of the Trinity in Roman Catholic theology. His axiom that "the economic Trinity is the immanent Trinity and the immanent Trinity is the economic Trinity" challenged the common tendency to privilege the one substance of God over the three persons. Rahner is critical of Augustine's "psychological theory of the Trinity" because, in his view, it overlooks the human experience of the economy of salvation in favor of speculations about the inner workings of the life of God ([1978] 2005, p. 135). His own pneumatology is shaped by his conviction that God is present in graceful "mediated immediacy" to each person. God is the Holy Mystery that grounds, conditions, and orients human subjectivity. In *Foundations of Christian Faith,* Rahner states that, "Insofar as he has come as the salvation which divinizes us in the inner-most center of the existence of the individual person, we call him really and truly 'Holy Spirit' or 'Holy Ghost'" ([1978] 2005, p. 136). Rahner's emphasis on the universality of the Spirit's self-communicating presence has often been appropriated for ecumenical and interreligious dialogue. His understanding of the eschatological presence of God as the Absolute Future also had an influence on several later pneumatological proposals, such as that of Denis Edwards, whom we will discuss below.

Sergius Bulgakov is widely considered the leading Eastern Orthodox theologian of the twentieth century, but many of his works have only recently been translated into English. His most extensive treatment of the Holy Spirit is *The Comforter* (2004). Bulgakov's entire theology involves an emphasis on the Divine Sophia, which he spells out in explicitly trinitarian terms. He appreciates Athanasius' emphasis on the dyadic action of the Son and the Spirit in the work of "Divine-humanity." However, he believes that his christological insights must be balanced with fresh attention to the relation between the Spirit and the Father. In his treatment of the procession of the Spirit, Bulgakov is critical not only of the Western anti-Photian doctrine of *filioque* but also the Eastern anti-*filioque* response, because he interprets both as caught up in a debate over the doctrine of causality in God. Instead of an emphasis on a causality of "mechanical unalterability," which is where most discussions of "origination" and "production" in the Trinity have led, he speaks of the Son and Spirit as two "images" of the Father's self-revealing love (pp. 136-37). Bulgakov also pays special attention to the ontological difference between the hypostases, which are supra-eternally posited in their differentiated unity as persons (not causes). The emphases on relationality and personality (over substance and causality) already evident here are played out in various ways among other Eastern theologians whom we have already treated (e.g., Lossky, 1998, and Zizioulas, 1985, 2006).

Part IV of Paul Tillich's *Systematic Theology* is titled "Life and the Spirit." Consistent with his overall approach of correlating human existential questions with the answers of the Christian gospel, he writes of "spirit" first of all as a dimension of human existence, which involves self-integration, self-creativity, and self-transcendence. Tillich then develops a pneumatology in which the divine Spirit is understood as the Spiritual Presence that grasps and calls the human spirit toward this actualization. He is especially attentive to the ambiguity of this experience of the dimension of life, and argues that the traditional trinitarian symbols may need to be replaced or complemented with new symbols that better express the manifestation of the divine life to humanity in contemporary culture. Tillich also criticizes the Western tendency to subordinate Spirit to Word, which he finds even in his own Lutheran tradition. Christology cannot be complete without pneumatology, for "the actualization of the New Being in history is the work of the Spirit" (1963, p. 285). Recognizing why in his own context Luther needed to stress the "Word alone," Tillich explicitly states that the whole of Part IV in his system is "a defense of the ecstatic manifestations of the Spiritual Presence against its ecclesiastical critics" (p. 118). However, he is also careful to resist the dangers of spiritual enthusiasm that places too much focus on the inner movements of the soul, because the divine Spirit's "invasion of the human spirit does not occur in isolated individuals but in social groups, since all the functions of the human spirit . . . are conditioned by the social context of the ego-thou encounter" (p. 139).

Wolfhart Pannenberg is another Lutheran theologian who has contributed to the revival of academic interest in the Holy Spirit. In Volume II of his *Systematic Theology* (1994), he suggests that we should "think of the dynamic of the divine Spirit as a working field linked to time and space — to time by the power of the future that gives creatures their own present and duration, and to space by the simultaneity of creatures in their duration. From the standpoint of the creature, origin from the future of the Spirit has the appearance of the past. But the working of the Spirit constantly encounters the creature as its future, which embraces its origin and its possible fulfilment" (p. 102). At least two themes in this synopsis are worth noting. First, Pannenberg was among the first theologians to appropriate the scientific concept of fields of force, developed by nineteenth-century physicists James Clerk Maxwell and Michael Faraday, for the reconstructive articulation of Christian pneumatology. He explores the relation between the creative presence of the divine Spirit and the general concept of energy fields as well as the particular human experience of openness to the future in several of the essays in *Toward a Theology of Nature* (1993). Although this move has been highly controversial, it has been appropriated and refigured by several other theologians, including Michael Welker, whom we will discuss below. Second, Pannenberg's understanding of the Spirit as the "power of the future" illustrates the attempt to move beyond past-oriented and mechanical conceptions of causality in pneumatology.

Pneumatology plays a role in virtually all of Jürgen Moltmann's works, but his most detailed treatment appears in *The Spirit of Life* (2001). For Moltmann, the Spirit is understood as the immanent and active presence of God in and to the world, penetrating and calling all of creation toward consummation. Yet he pays special attention in this book to the human experience of life, which is interpreted theologically as life "in the Spirit." As elsewhere, here Moltmann emphasizes the way in which the Spirit brings salvation not simply by altering the individual soul but by liberating the whole community into new forms of life-giving fellowship. The universal coming of God is a dominant theme for Moltmann's theology, and like Pannenberg he understands the divine Spirit as mediating the arrival of the future, although he spells this out differently. Unlike Barth and many of his other Reformed predecessors, Moltmann unambiguously embraces the use of the term "person" for the Spirit. Rejecting Boethius's definition of person (with its reliance on the concept of individual rational substance), he argues that personality and relationality are genetically connected. However, the ways in which the personhood of the Spirit, Son, and Father are formed in relation to one another are not identical. For Moltmann, "The personhood of God the Holy Spirit is the loving, self-communicating, out-fanning, and out-pouring presence of the eternal divine life of the triune God" (p. 289). His primary objection to the *filioque* is that it fails to account for the biblical witness, in which the Spirit accompanies, rests in, and shines from the Son (p. 308).

In *God the Spirit* (1994), Michael Welker's overall project is to provide an interpretation of experiences of God's Spirit that both takes account of the diverse biblical testimonies and engages the skepticism of the contemporary world. The book begins with the problem of talking realistically about experiencing the Spirit in a global context where, on the one hand, God is typically conceived (if at all) as distant, while, on the other hand, movements such as liberation, feminist, and Pentecostal theology emphasize the immanence of God. After outlining early (relatively unclear) biblical testimonies about the Spirit, Welker points to (chronologically) later texts in Scripture that link the Spirit's power to justice and peace. He argues that the life and ministry of Jesus Christ reveal the concrete presence of the Spirit of truth and of love, and describes the outpouring of the Spirit as an action of liberation and of overcoming the world. Far from a means of escape from responsibility in the world, Welker depicts the Spirit as a "force field" or "domain of resonance" into which people are called and bound together in love and peace. In the final chapter, he urges a move beyond Aristotelian and Hegelian concepts of Spirit, and invites us to think of the "public person" of the Spirit, who is "God in the midst of creation." In addition to building on resources from his own Reformed tradition, Welker has also drawn from and promoted wider ecumenical dialogue. He recently edited a book on *The Work of the Spirit: Pneumatology and Pentecostalism* (2006), and several of the essays in this volume are annotated in Part II (below).

Throughout the twentieth century and into the twenty-first, several theologians have participated in the renewal and refiguration of "Spirit-christology," that is, ways of understanding the mission of Jesus Christ as in some sense constituted by the active presence of the Holy Spirit (cf. Del Colle, 1994). This movement was facilitated by the broader revival of trinitarian doctrine we have already mentioned. In his contribution to *Advents of the Spirit* (2001), David Coffey argues that Spirit-christology is the best mode of access to a theology of the Trinity. He does not follow those early church fathers for whom the term "Spirit" in this phrase refers simply to the divine element in Christ (as opposed to the human or fleshly element). Rather, it is the presence of the third person of the Trinity that constitutes the whole personhood of Jesus. Coffey draws here on some texts from Augustine and Cyril of Alexandria, which hint that the Incarnation can be understood as the Father's radical gift of the Holy Spirit to the humanity of Christ. He argues that Spirit-christology can and should incorporate (while going beyond) the insights of *Logos* christology, which focuses on understanding the mystery of the Incarnation basically in terms of the hypostatic union between the divine *Logos* and the human Jesus, with little or no appeal to the Holy Spirit. Coffey argues that some such radical refiguring of categories will be required to move beyond the ecumenical impasse in the *filioque* debate.

One of the favorite phrases of Lutheran theologian Robert Jenson is that Pentecost is a peer of Easter, and it indicates his interest in developing a theological approach that emphasizes pneumatology as strongly as christology. Like Moltmann and Pannenberg, although with a style all his own, Jenson develops his doctrine of the Holy Spirit with special attention to the idea of the futurity of God. In his essay "What is the Point of Trinitarian Theology?" (1995), Jenson summarizes his position: "the Spirit is God as the Power of his own and our future; and it is that the Spirit is God as the Power of his own future, as the Power of a future that is truly 'unexpected' and yet connected, also for him, that the Spirit is a distinct identity of and in God" (p. 41). While Jenson retains the Eastern Orthodox emphasis on the Father as the *archē* (ground or source) of the Godhead, he also wants to argue that the Holy Spirit is the end (or *telos*) of all God's ways. The "temporal infinity" of God is the unsurpassability of the event of the Spirit as God who comes to us from the last future. Jenson spells this out in more detail in the first volume of his *Systematic Theology* (1997). The Spirit is "at the End of all God's ways because he is the End of all God's ways. The Spirit is the Liveliness of the divine life because he is the Power of the divine future." The Spirit is the one as whom God is future to himself, the person of the Trinity who "liberates God the Father from himself . . . to be the actual *archē* of deity." The Spirit not only liberates the Father for the Son, but also liberates the Son "from and for the Father," who as the one who is begotten and liberated "reconciles the Father with the future his Spirit is" (pp. 157-61).

The Roman Catholic theologian Denis Edwards illustrates several of the themes we have already observed. In his *Breath of Life: A Theology of the Creator Spirit* (2004), Edwards places his reconstruction of the doctrine of the Spirit in the context of the whole history of the evolving and expanding universe. He describes the Spirit as "the immanent divine principle" that enables the cosmos to evolve by breathing life into a universe of creatures (p. 34). Building on Basil of Caesarea's idea of the Holy Spirit as the one who brings all things to perfection, Edwards emphasizes the dynamic eschatological presence of the Spirit who enfolds all human beings in grace, brings about the Christ event, and draws the church into communion with God. He also appropriates Karl Rahner's emphasis on God as the "Absolute Future" of all creation, but attempts to develop this insight further in terms of an explicitly trinitarian theology of the Spirit of God (p. 46). The creator Spirit is not construed primarily as the "will" of God that forces creatures along a predetermined timeline, but an intimate presence that is "making all things new" by calling them to share in the eternal trinitarian life. Critical of the West's privileging of the Word over Spirit in many of its interpretations of the *filioque,* Edwards suggests that we affirm both that the Word is fully involved in the procession of the Spirit *and* that the Spirit proceeds from the Source of All (the Mother/Father) *through* the Word. Moreover, he insists that the Spirit is "fully involved with the generation of The Word" and "eternally *rests upon* the Word" (pp. 150-53), in order to reinforce the claim that they are eternally coexistent and reciprocally related in the eternal life of the trinitarian God.

For the sake of space, we have deferred a summary of some of the other twentieth-century developments in pneumatology to the annotated bibliography in Part II. There the reader will find resources for exploring a variety of interpretations of the transforming experience of the Holy Spirit, including pneumatological proposals that engage or retrieve theological aesthetics (von Balthasar, 1993; Sherry, 2002), mystical theology (McIntosh, 1998; Sheldrake, 1998), and process philosophy (Reynolds, 1990).

Throughout this brief introduction to the doctrine of the Holy Spirit we have tried to emphasize the way in which the interpretation of the experience of transformation among Christians is embedded within and shaped by particular cultural contexts and ecclesial concerns. On the one hand, formulations of this doctrine are intended to articulate the biblical intuitions about the evocative, life-giving power of the *ruach* of Yahweh and the *pneuma* of the One who raised Christ from the dead. On the other hand, the process of conserving the illuminating and liberating power of the biblical tradition requires of every theological generation that it critically engage the plausibility structures of its own social context. Where do we go from here?

Transforming Pneumatology

In this final section we explore the future of the doctrine of the Holy Spirit. Our goal is not to set out a new constructive proposal, but simply to indicate some of the directions we anticipate pneumatological reflection might go in light of the tensions and trajectories we have explored in this book. As we have seen, Christian theologians have always been confronted with the need for reconstructing pneumatology. The church of the twenty-first century will also have to take up this ongoing task of interpreting the experience of the Spirit of the biblical God. This is the first sense in which we mean "transforming pneumatology" — reconstructing the formulations of the doctrine. However, we also want to suggest that this exercise is not merely academic, for the way in which we talk about the Spirit can itself facilitate — or fail to facilitate — our own transformation. We can ask not only how pneumatology might be transformed in the future but also how we might be transformed through our attempts to interpret our experience of the divine Spirit.

Although it is intertwined with worship and praxis, Christian theology is a conceptual endeavor, and so for the sake of this concluding section it makes sense to organize a presentation of possible new directions in pneumatology around the conceptual shifts that we have observed throughout the book. These shifts are tied to the three philosophical categories we identified in the Introduction: matter, person, and force. As we have seen, these have had a particularly significant role in formulations of the doctrine of the Holy Spirit throughout the history of the church. It makes sense to expect, therefore, that whatever new directions pneumatology takes in the twenty-first, century, it will need to engage developments in late modern philosophy, science, and culture that shape the meaning and use of these concepts. Many of the general theological movements and particular pneumatological proposals outlined in the last few sections have not only engaged such developments, but actively participated in the reconstructive process. Although the following three shifts are woven together creatively in the fabric of so much contemporary theology, we are distinguishing between them here for the sake of aiding in our conceptual analysis.

First, we have observed that the dichotomy between matter and spirit, understood as two kinds of substance, has been increasingly challenged in recent theology. Insofar as the concept of "spirit" was defined negatively in distinction from "matter" (as immaterial substance), it was difficult for theologians to make sense of the relation of the divine Spirit to the material world without inappropriately setting them side by side (as in the eighteenth-century philosophy of deism, in which God and the world do not interact) or conflating them into one substance (as in pantheism, in which all is God and God is all). Most late modern philosophers and scientists no longer rely on this metaphysical distinction in their interpretations of human experience of the world. For example, in contemporary physics matter itself is no longer conceptualized in terms of extended atomic substances that bump into each other in absolute space. What we call matter are constellations of knots within the fields of energy that constitute the space-time continuum. Albert Einstein's recognition that "matter" and "energy" are transferable ($E=mc^2$) has made it possible for theorists in the sciences of emergent complexity to conceptualize what has traditionally been called "spirit" (or "form" or "life") as in some sense a qualification of matter. In other words, spirit is related to matter in some *positive* way without being simply reducible to it.

As we have seen, many of the constructive proposals in twentieth-century pneumatology have been motivated by the pernicious effects of matter/spirit dualism, and have attempted to interpret the experience of spiritual transformation in different ways. This was particularly evident among feminist and liberation theologians who challenged the traditional tendency to depict the work of the Spirit primarily in relation to the sanctification of the soul, which often was associated with a deferral of hope for embodied transformation to the hereafter. The affirmation of matter in pneumatology is also illustrated in Eugene Rogers's *After the Spirit: A Constructive Pneumatology from Resources Outside the Modern West* (2005). Rogers argues that "to think about the Spirit, you have to think materially, because, in Christian terms, the Spirit has befriended matter" (p. 58). Although this has implications for all of creation, this befriending of matter is revealed primarily in the Spirit's resting upon the *body* of the Son, which Rogers depicts graphically in relation to the womb of Mary, the waters of baptism, and the bread of the Eucharist, as well as the transfiguration of society and all of creation. The way in which the need for reconstructing pneumatology is increasingly linked to the ecological crisis also illustrates this shift (cf. Wallace, 1996). While these developments in the concept of matter clearly challenge many traditional formulations, they have also provided an opportunity for Christian theologians to retrieve ways of linking the Spirit to the transformation of all of creation already anticipated in the communion of those liberated through fellowship in the Spirit.

The second category that is particularly important for pneumatology is the concept of person. It is difficult to overemphasize the influence of Boethius's definition of person as "an individual substance of a rational nature" on Christian theology in general and the doctrine of the Spirit in particular. This way of conceptualizing personhood was shaped in part by Augustine, who emphasized the powers (faculties) of the intellect and will in the individual soul. As we have seen, this anthropological model shaped formulations of the relation of the Spirit to the Father and the Son (the *filioque* debates). In late modern philosophy and psychology, however, every aspect of Boethius's definition has been challenged. Today, human personhood is understood as emerging within and mediated through the relationality of interpersonal and social systems. Neuroscientists have shown that rationality and emotion (which is embodied) are integrated in the human organism. To be a person is to be in relation, and these relations are not reducible to one's intellectual (or volitional) faculties. Although the term "spirit" was almost excised from the vocabulary of anthropology in the middle of the twentieth century, given its association with some forms of vitalism (that is, the belief in a mysterious "vital energy" that exists apart from scientific laws), a growing number of philosophers and scientists are refiguring the concept by relating it to holistic experience of human life in dynamic relation to others.

This shift in the category of "person" has rather obvious implications for the way in which we articulate the relations of the Holy Spirit to the Father and Son in the doctrine of the Trinity. As we have seen in the last three sections, more relational conceptions of personhood have increasingly played a central role in the pneumatological reflections of many of the leading theologians of the twentieth century — Eastern Orthodox, Roman Catholic, and Protestant alike. Progress in the dialogue over the *filioque* clause has been dependent in large part on the conceptual space opened up by fresh attention to the complexity of relationality among divine and human persons. Moreover, the communal dimension of personal existence has also contributed to the ecclesial and social emphases within feminist and liberation treatments of the Spirit in particular and the Trinity in general. We could also point again to Michael Welker's notion of the public personhood of the Spirit, who may be conceived as a "field of force" that constitutes public force fields and generates a "domain of resonance" into which embodied human persons are liberated and invited to orient themselves toward others in concrete acts of love. This proposal also illustrates the intrinsic link between philosophical shifts in the concept of person and shifts in the concepts of force and matter.

The concept of force (or power) is the third philosophical category that we have argued plays a special role in the doctrine of the Holy Spirit. When the concept of movement could be explained by Platonic active immaterial principles or by Aristotelian entelechies and final causes, it was relatively easy to conceptualize the role of the "spiritual" as a force in the cosmos. In classical mechanics, however, force was understood in terms of the impact of masses (material substances) on the inertial frame of other masses, whose acceleration and distance could be measured in the context of absolute space and time. The formula $F=ma$ (that is, force equals mass times acceleration) leaves little room — or none — for the divine Spirit to fit into such a linear chain of determined mechanical causes. When theology was dominated by a past-oriented concept of force, it was tempting to fit the power of the Spirit into the same kind of deterministic scheme that explained all other changes, leading to a focus on the ordered movement of individual souls through the "states" of salvation — the so-called *ordo salutis*. In late modernity we can trace a shift away from early modern mechanistic and linear conceptions of natural motion, which focused primarily on the efficiency of past causes that determine present and future effects. When mass and motion (velocity) were integrated within fields of energy ($E=mc^2$), this opened up new possibilities for conceptualizing the human experience of temporality and causation.

As we have seen, many twentieth-century theologians have taken advantage of this opportunity in their reconstructive pneumatological efforts. For example, the linking of the Spirit to the power of the future, to the eschatological presence of God that opens up space and time for creaturely coming-to-be, was at the generative core of the proposals of thinkers as diverse as Rahner, Moltmann, Pannenberg, and Zizioulas. The interpretation of the experience of the Spirit as the agency of God who is now making present the coming reign of divine peace has also been appropriated by feminist and liberation theologians in their concern for empowerment. We can also point to Bernard Cooke's recent *Power and the Spirit of God* (2004), which engages social scientific critiques of power and proposes a new emphasis on the embrace of the Spirit. He argues that developments in the late modern conceptualization of power represent "what may be the most radical shift in mentality to touch Christianity in eighteen hundred years" (p. 7). In contrast to the forceful and coercive plays of power in public life, which postmodern analysis has unveiled, Cooke wants to emphasize the eschatological and life-giving power of the Spirit. As a final example, we mention Sigurd Bergmann, whose *Creation Set Free: The Spirit as Liberator of Nature* (2005) appropriates Gregory of Nazianzus's cosmic pneumatology to illustrate all three shifts: an emphasis on the Spirit's indwelling of corporeal human beings, on the Spirit's enhancement of community and on the Spirit's vivification and consummation of the cosmos (pp. 154-55).

What are we to make of these trends and where do we go from here? We have not tried to hide our enthusiasm for each of these conceptual shifts. One key criterion for evaluation is the extent to which our formulations in the doctrine of the Holy Spirit facilitate the transformation of our spiritual practices. Our interest in "*transforming* pneumatology" is motivated not only by the need for conceptual reformulation, but also by the hope that our speech about the Spirit might function transformatively in the church and the world. Judgments about the success of particular proposals and practices will be shaped by our own embodied and social contexts, but we can search together for ways to recover and refigure the intuitions of the biblical tradition as we engage contemporary philosophy, science, and culture in dialogue. We believe that some aspects of these conceptual shifts in ways of thinking about matter, person, and force can help facilitate the integration of the doctrine of the Spirit and the practice of spirituality in our late modern context:

- First, a pneumatology in which the divine Spirit is understood as an all-embracing and all-pervading dynamic presence, in which all creaturely spatio-temporal forms of energized "material" live and move and have their being, invites more relational, holistic, and embodied practices in spirituality.
- Second, a pneumatology in which the divine Spirit is understood as eternally with, for, and in communal relation vis-à-vis the Father and the Son, welcoming creatures to participate in the divine communion, invites models of spirituality that tend more carefully to the social formation of persons.
- Third, a pneumatology in which the divine Spirit is understood as the promising presence of Eternity to time, constituting the creaturely ex-

perience of temporality precisely by calling all things to share in the absolute Beauty of God, invites the exploration of forms of spiritual life in which the opening up of the future is interpreted as pure gift, liberating persons as agents of hope in the world.

Nevertheless, each of these conceptual shifts brings challenges as well as opportunities. Theology must appropriate them critically. And so as we orient ourselves toward reconstructing pneumatology in our contemporary context, we conclude by identifying three critical tasks that face us. These pneumatological issues are not isolated from the overall process of reconstructing systematic theology, which means that a full treatment would need to attend to ways in which developments in the doctrine of God, theological anthropology, and other themes also shape our work in the doctrine of the Holy Spirit (cf. Shults & Sandage, 2006, Part I).

The first critical task will be to ensure that presentations of a Christian understanding of the relation between God and the world that overcome the problems of dualism (or deism) do not inadvertently collapse into monism (or pantheism) by simply conflating the concepts of Spirit and matter. We are helped in this case by the twentieth-century retrieval of apophatic theology, with its careful refusal to conceptualize God, or the divine Spirit, as one type of being or substance defined in comparison with or in contrast to creaturely beings (or creaturely being itself). If we think of divine Infinity only in terms of indefinite extension of creaturely attributes, or as the negation of finitude, then we would have a concept of the Infinite that was itself limited by its determination in relation to the finite, which is to say, itself finite. Speaking of the divine Spirit as truly Infinite in relation to the (energized-spatial-temporal) material world can help us imaginatively interpret our experience of that intensely disturbing and comforting incomparable presence that is closer to us than we are to ourselves.

Another critical task will be presenting pneumatology in a way that avoids not only the modalist tendencies of psychological models of the Trinity, but also the tri-theistic leanings of some of the social trinitarian models that have emerged in the last half century. Here we ought to move beyond thinking of the three "persons" of the Trinity as three repetitions of the same kind of rational individual, who happen to take different roles. The way in which human creatures are called to be "persons" follows the form of the "personality" of the eternal Son, which was manifested in the life of Jesus of Nazareth — facing the eternal Father in faithful, loving, and hopeful dependence on the eternal Spirit. We can still speak of the perichoretic being-in-relation of the Father and the Spirit as "personal," but the way in which they are mutually present to, in, and for one another and the Son *is* the eternal ground of the evocation of the human experience of personality — not simply two more examples of it (cf. Shults, 2005, p. 163).

The third critical task that emerges in light of our analysis is depicting the power of the divine Spirit in a way that escapes the constraints of early modern fatalism (the view that all things are predetermined) and voluntarism (an emphasis on the efficacy of the will, divine and human) without giving up on the idea of God as the absolute ground of all things. Here we commend the late modern renewal of eschatological ontology, the intuition that in some sense creaturely *being* is constituted by the *coming* of God. The so-called turn to futurity has its own implicit dangers, such as the temptation to speak of a reversal of causation that collapses into postdeterminism. Nevertheless, we might find resources in this conceptual shift for articulating a reformative pneumatology in the context of an overarching understanding of the Creator as the One from whom, through whom, *and to whom* all things are (Rom. 11:36). Such a doctrine of the Holy Spirit will want to maintain that the trinitarian God is the ultimate origin of all things precisely *as* the conditioning goal of all things.

These new directions in transforming pneumatology are commendable for another reason. They may quicken in us a sense of hope that the doctrine of the Holy Spirit may itself come to be articulated in a way that is *inherently* gospel. The disturbing and comforting presence of the Spirit of the trinitarian God is good news indeed, for our embodied desire for an open future of peaceful communion is constituted, upheld, and fulfilled by this all-embracing advent of the infinitely life-giving eschatological force that renews all things by calling them into a transformative participation in the life of Eternity.

Come Holy Spirit

II. ENGLISH-LANGUAGE RESOURCES
ON THE HOLY SPIRIT

The goal of Part I of this book was to provide an introductory outline of the broad themes and historical developments in the Christian doctrine of the Holy Spirit. Part II is designed to help the reader who is interested in exploring one or more of these aspects of pneumatology in more detail. We have limited ourselves to treatments of the Holy Spirit that are available in the English language, with occasional reference to where translated works may be found in their original languages. For many patristic writers the easiest place to find their treatments of the Holy Spirit are in multivolume sets, the most common of which are abbreviated as ANF (Ante-Nicene Fathers) and NPNF1 and NPNF2 (Nicene and Post-Nicene Fathers, first and second series).

The complex, diverse, and uneven nature of the literature on this doctrine makes it difficult to divide a bibliography into clear sections. Even the common distinction between "primary" and "secondary" literature is not so easily made in this case, where historical and constructive pneumatological reflections are so often woven together. For this reason, we have decided simply to list all of the bibliographic references by author in alphabetical order, and to let the index do the work of helping the reader find resources on any particular theme of interest (e.g., *filioque*, Gregory of Nyssa, feminism). Readers may be surprised to find some major works/authors treated briefly in this section. Normally this brevity is due to the fact that they were treated more thoroughly in the historical overview of Part I. Here again, the index will help the reader locate the appropriate place in the text.

Annotated Bibliography

Albrecht, Daniel. *Rites in the Spirit: A Ritual Approach to Pentecostal/Charismatic Spirituality.* Sheffield: Sheffield Academic Press, 1999.

Albrecht argues that the experience of the immanent, active presence of the Spirit is at the core of Pentecostal and charismatic spirituality. After an overview of the history of these movements, he offers an in-depth analysis of their characteristic spiritual practices. Using three churches as case studies, he interprets these forms of spirituality through the lens of ritual studies, highlighting their symbolic, liturgical, and iconic aspects.

Ambrose of Milan. *On the Holy Spirit.* NPNF2, vol. 10. Peabody, Mass.: Hendrickson, 1994.

This treatise by Ambrose (340-397 A.D.) is one of the earliest comprehensive Latin treatises on the Holy Spirit. The bishop of Milan argues for the full deity of the Spirit by establishing that, like the Father and the Son, the Spirit is not a creature. His proposal illustrates a common tension in the Western tradition: on the one hand, the Spirit is divine, which he takes to mean an unchanging, incorporeal substance, which is "separated from association" with the created order (I.5.75; p. 103). On the other hand, in our experience of salvation the Spirit seems present to us. Ambrose insists that although the Spirit "seems to come down" to us in reality "He does not come down," rather, "our mind ascends to Him" (I.11.121; p. 109). Ambrose's most important pupil was Augustine.

Anderson, Allan. *An Introduction to Pentecostalism: Global Charismatic Christianity.* Cambridge: Cambridge University Press, 2004.

This book provides an overview of the historical development of the worldwide Pentecostal and charismatic movements in Christianity. Anderson points out the complexity of the origins and diversity of expression in these movements. He interprets the Azusa Street revival as only one among many charismatic revivals that erupted across the globe during the first decade of the twentieth century. Arguing that "the experience of the fullness of the Spirit is the essence of Pentecostal and Charismatic theology" (p. 196), this book illustrates the connection between Spirit-centered theology and experience.

Arnett, William M. "The Role of the Holy Spirit in Entire Sanctification in the Writings of John Wesley." *Wesleyan Theological Journal* 14, no. 2 (Fall 1979): 15-30.

This article provides a survey of Wesley's understanding of the Spirit with special reference to the idea of sanctification. Arnett's claim that sanctification was for Wesley the broadest category for understanding the work of the Holy Spirit is supported by quotations from a variety of his works. This essay clarifies Wesley's understanding of the preparatory work of and baptism "with" the Holy Spirit.

Athanasius. "Letters to Serapion." In *The Letters of Saint Athanasius Concerning the Holy Spirit,* translated by C. R. B. Shapland. London: Epworth Press, 1951.

These letters explicitly defended the deity of the Spirit against the neo-Arians who argued that the Spirit (like the Son) is a creature. The term *homoousios,* which Athanasius had championed at Nicea with reference to the Son, he utilizes here with reference to the Holy Spirit. "But because [the Spirit] is one, and, still more, because he is proper to the Word who is one, he is proper to God who is one, and one in essence [*homoousios*] with him" (I.27; p. 133). He also argues that since only God can sanctify and deify, and since that is precisely the work of the Spirit in believers, the Spirit must be God.

Augustine of Hippo. *The Trinity.* Translated by Edmund Hill. Brooklyn: New City Press, 1991.

This text is one of the most influential for Western pneumatology, playing an important role in the inclusion of the *filioque* clause in later liturgical debates. Augustine emphasizes that the Holy Spirit is the Spirit of the Father and the Son, and as such, is the Gift and Love of both which proceeds eternally as "a kind of inexpressible communion or fellowship of Father and Son" (V.3.12; p. 197). In this treatise he also spells out his famous "psychological" analogy which suggests that just as the human soul is comprised of memory, intellect, and will (but is nevertheless one substance), we can think of God as one immaterial substance, and connect the Father with memory, the Son with intellect, and the Spirit with will (XV; pp. 395-443). Augustine deals with pneumatology, directly or indirectly, in several other works, including *Confessions, On the Spirit and the Letter, City of God,* and *Enchiridion.*

Badcock, Gary D. *Light of Truth and Fire of Love: A Theology of the Holy Spirit.* Grand Rapids: Eerdmans, 1997.

Critical of what he sees as a lack of balance between Word and Spirit in much recent theology, Badcock attempts to outline a more subtle reciprocal relation between christology and pneumatology. He develops his argument in the context of an overview of historical interpretations of the Spirit, including chapters on biblical perspectives on the Spirit, the patristic consensus, the *filioque* controversy, and the Reformation tradition, with special attention on Luther and Calvin. Badcock's proposal formally links the articulation of pneumatology to the experience of the Spirit, calling for an integration of orthodoxy and orthopraxis in Spirit-doctrine. As the title indicates, his material argument for integrating Word and Spirit centers around the biblical emphasis on and Christian experience of truth and love.

Balthasar, Hans Urs von. "The Unknown Lying Beyond the Word." In *Explorations in Theology,* vol. 3, *Creator Spirit,* translated by B. McNeill, C.R.V. San Francisco: Ignatius, 1993.

Although pneumatological concerns are woven throughout his many works, and are especially prominent in his massive trilogy in systematics, this small but important essay is frequently quoted by contemporary von Balthasar scholars seeking to demonstrate the relation between his theological aesthetics and the doctrine of the Spirit. In it, Balthasar suggests that as the "unknown beyond the Word," the Holy Spirit allows us to, in faith, "let go of the handrail of the Word, so that we can walk without vertigo in the sphere of freedom; only in believing hope dare we join Peter in leaving the ship to venture out into the billowing infinity of the divine Spirit" (p. 111). In von Balthasar's thought the Holy Spirit is the eternal divine witness to radical otherness, both in the sense of otherness between the Father and the Son, and otherness between the human person and God. This leads him to speak of the Holy Spirit as mediator, dynamic space, and love which spans the yawning gulf between radically opposed poles. The Spirit indwells us as divine witness, and gives us the ability to perceive the beauty of Christ and be drawn into the infinite trinitarian life of God.

Barrois, Georges. "Two Styles of Theology and Spirituality." *St. Vladimir's Theological Quarterly* 26, no. 2 (1982): 89-102.

Barrois summarizes the differences in styles between "the West," which is especially indebted to Augustine and Thomas, and "the East," which is more heavily influenced by the Cappadocians and Gregory of Palamas. His goal in this context is not to argue that one approach is better than the other, but to demonstrate how theological decisions on the nature of the Holy Spirit, and deeper philosophical decisions about substance and energy, also shape the way in which spirituality is understood and practiced.

Barth, Karl. *Church Dogmatics.* Translated and edited by G. W. Bromiley and T. F. Torrance. 4 vols. Edinburgh: T&T Clark, 1936-1969.

This is generally considered one of the most important theological works of the twentieth century. Although Barth never wrote the fifth volume, which would have focused on the Holy Spirit, he does deal with pneumatological issues in the other volumes, especially in volume 1 (in the context of the Trinity) and in volume 4 (in the context of the doctrine of reconciliation).

Basil of Caesarea. *On the Holy Spirit.* Translated by Blomfield Jackson. NPNF2, vol. 8. Peabody, Mass.: Hendrickson, 1994.

This is one of the most important contributions of the Cappadocian Fathers to pneumatology. Basil's analysis and clarification of the doctrine of the Spirit is integrated within his pastoral concern to outline in detail the gifts and graces bestowed by the Breath of Life, which transform human life. See especially the following sections: XIII.30; XVI.38; XVIII.45-48; XXV.59; XXVIII.70; and XXX.77.

Bergmann, Sigurd. *Creation Set Free: The Spirit as Liberator of Nature.* Grand Rapids: Eerdmans, 2005.

This pneumatological proposal is constructed in light of contemporary concerns about ecology and liberation and in dialogue with classical patristic resources, especially Gregory of Nazianzus. Bergmann appropriates Gregory's understanding of the role of the Spirit as leading "God and creation ever closer together" (p. 171) in order to emphasize the Spirit's role as redeemer of the cosmos. He outlines an ecological pneumatology of liberation that "reconstructs the Nicene Creed — specifically the confession to the Spirit of triunity as the creator of life and the coming world — such that the Spirit, rather than functioning as the mediator between the Father/Son and the world, appears instead as the triune God who acts at places within a world in need of redemption" (p. 358).

Bernard of Clairvaux. *On the Song of Songs.* In *Bernard of Clairvaux: Selected Works,* translated by G. R. Evans. New York: Paulist, 1987.

Bernard was a twelfth-century Cistercian abbot who emphasized desire, contemplation, and the soul's journey to God in his writings. In Sermon 8 of this commentary, he speaks of the Holy Spirit as the kiss of the Father received by the Son, and declares that through contemplation and reception of this kiss, it is possible for the soul to experience union with God in contemplative marriage, and participate in the life of the Trinity.

Boff, Leonardo. *Church: Charism and Power: Liberation Theology and the Institutional Church.* Translated by John W. Diercksmeier. New York: Crossroad, 1985.

This book provides an example of the tendency among liberation theologians to emphasize the surprising and empowering charismata of the Spirit in relation to the power structures of ecclesial institutions.

―――. *Holy Trinity, Perfect Community.* Translated by Phillip Berryman. Maryknoll, N.Y.: Orbis Books, 1988.

This book depicts the Trinity as an egalitarian community and encourages forms of ecclesial organization that value the gifts of the Spirit among all members.

Bonaventure. *The Soul's Journey to God.* Translated by E. Cousins. Nw York: Paulist, 1978.

In this influential medieval treatise, a Franciscan mystical theologian describes the process of the soul's entry into spiritual union with God.

Breck, John. *Spirit of Truth: The Origins of Johannine Pneumatology.* Crestwood, N.Y.: St. Vladimir's Seminary Press, 1991.

Breck divides his treatment of the origins of John's understanding of the Spirit into two parts. Part I examines "The Spirit in the Old Testament and Ancient Near East," and emphasizes the development of Israel's religious consciousness, which affected its interpretation of the Spirit in its salvation history. He also outlines other ancient Near Eastern religions' concept of spirit, such as the Egyptian *ka,* the Sumero-Akkadian idea of *sharu* ("wind" or "life-breath"), and the Iranian (Zoroastrian) understanding of *Mainyu,* the "Bounteous Spirit" or "Spirit of Truth." In Part II Breck explores the concept of the Spirit in the Hellenistic Age, beginning with the sources and development of the Jewish wisdom tradition and the linking of the Spirit *(ruach)* to wisdom *(chochma).* He also outlines the classical Greek usage of the concept of *pneuma* in the mystery religions and hermetic thought of the first century. His final chapter examines the Dead Sea Scrolls and explores the similarities and differences between the Scrolls' dualistic understanding of the "Spirit of Truth" and the "Spirit of the Lie" and that of the Iranians. Breck concludes with a summary of the way in which pre-Christian Jewish documents tend to see the function of the divine Spirit as both revelatory and soteriological, and he hints at the ways in which these emphases will be taken up and refigured in the New Testament.

Buckley, James J., and David S. Yeago, eds. *Knowing the Triune God: The Work of the Spirit in the Practices of the Church.* Grand Rapids: Eerdmans, 2001.

Two of the essays in this volume pay particular attention to the way in which the doctrine of the Spirit shapes the practices of the church. The first is Reinhard Hütter's chapter on "The Church" (pp. 23-47). Retrieving a traditional understanding of the church as the primary place in which we come to know God, he argues that this knowledge is received through the work of the Holy Spirit as we engage in embodied practices. Hütter is critical of Barth's pneumatology and calls for a more robust view of the Spirit, one that follows the lead of Eastern Orthodox thinkers like Zizioulas, in which the sanctifying work of the Spirit is understood as constitutive of and for the practices of the church, including its practice of theological discourse. The other essay that most directly engages pneumatology is Buckley's "The Wounded Body: The Spirit's Ecumenical Work on Divisions among Christians" (pp. 205-30). He suggests that the ecumenical movement can be aided by recognizing that its very existence is a work of the Spirit, who moves us toward participation and fellowship precisely in (and on) our wounded materiality, including our narratives, teachings, and practices. Buckley outlines a pneumatological interpretation of ecumenism that recovers traditional themes connected to the work of the Spirit, such as speaking through the prophets, teaching all things, and indwelling the wounded body of the church, calling it to new life.

Bulgakov, Sergius. *The Comforter.* Translated by Boris Jakim. Grand Rapids: Eerdmans, 2004.

This is the most exhaustive treatment of the doctrine of the Holy Spirit by one of the most influential twentieth-century Eastern Orthodox theologians.

Burgess, Stanley M. *The Holy Spirit.* 3 vols. Peabody, Mass.: Hendrickson, 1984-1997.

This trilogy is one of the few historical surveys specifically devoted to tracing the development of the doctrine of the Holy Spirit from the time of the early church through the Reformation (cf. Congar, 1997). Each book in the series is organized chronologically, and succinctly describes the life, writings, and pneumatological concerns of major Christian theologians. As a Pentecostal theologian, Burgess is careful to highlight the role of spiritual gifts in the interpretations and experiences of the Spirit throughout history.

The first volume, *Ancient Christian Traditions,* examines the Holy Spirit in the works of the early apostolic fathers to Augustine. It shows how the first five centuries of Christianity were both spiritually vibrant and theologically conflicted (especially in regard to the Trinity), and demonstrates how the church sought to resolve the tension between "prophecy" (e.g., visions and ecstasies) and "order" (e.g., creeds and institutions). In the second volume, *Eastern Christian Traditions,* Burgess seeks to show that the East developed a more prominent and nuanced pneumatology than did the West. As it emphasized perichoresis (mutuality among the Father, Son, and Spirit), theosis (deification), and mystical prayer, the Eastern church witnessed the emergence of a fecund and vital theology of the Holy Spirit in late antiquity and the medieval era. The final volume, *Medieval Roman Catholic and Reformation Traditions,* highlights the pneumatologies of major Western scholastics, mystics, and reformers, many of whom described the Spirit as the bond of love between Father and Son (following Augustine).

Burgess's clear and concise summaries of the key players and developments in the history of the doctrine of the Spirit make his trilogy one of the best starting points for further research in pneumatology. The second and third volumes also contain glossaries of relevant theological terms that will assist readers who are new to this dialogue.

Burgess, Stanley M., and Eduard M. van der Maas, eds. *The New International Dictionary of Pentecostal and Charismatic Movements.* Revised and Expanded Edition. Grand Rapids: Zondervan, 2002.

This is one of the most comprehensive resources currently available for understanding the history, global reach, and theologies of Pentecostalism. Part I is a survey of Pentecostalism in various countries and regions around the globe. Part II is a detailed statistical report of growth patterns for three historical "waves" of the movement: Pentecostal, charismatic, and neocharismatic. Part III is a dictionary containing concise summaries of key topics pertaining to Pentecostalism. Burgess's lengthy article on the doctrine of the Holy Spirit (pp. 730-69) is particularly helpful for gaining an overview of the development of pneumatology (from the church fathers through the reformers of the sixteenth century) from a distinctly Pentecostal perspective.

Calvin, John. *Institutes of the Christian Religion.* Edited by John T. McNeill. Translated by Ford Lewis Battles. Philadelphia: Westminster Press, 1960.

Originally published in 1551, this is a classical systematic presentation of Christian doctrine by the theologian many consider the father of the Reformed tradition. Calvin pays special attention to the Holy Spirit in the process of sanctification in volume III of the *Institutes.*

Catherine of Siena. *The Dialogue.* Translated by Suzanne Noffke. New York: Paulist, 1980.

Catherine of Siena (1347-1380), to whom the Roman Catholic Church granted the title "Doctor of the Church" in 1970, was a prominent medieval mystical theologian as well as a key player in the tumultuous world of late fourteenth-century Tuscan politics. Catherine's pneumatology is most evident in *The Dialogue* — her magnum opus, which was composed approximately two years before her death at the age of thirty-three. In agreement with Augustine, Thomas Aquinas, and Bernard of Clairvaux before her, Catherine speaks of the Holy Spirit as the "loving charity" between the Father and the Son, and also draws a close correlation between the three human psychological faculties of memory, understanding, and will and God's triune life as Father, Son, and Holy Spirit. The Spirit is linked with the transformation of the human will from a state of fearful selfishness to one of merciful love for God, others, and self. Catherine is known for her creative and multilayered theological metaphors. Some of her pneumatological imagery recasts themes already common to Christian Scripture and tradition; for example, she depicts the Holy Spirit as a flame of "burning love" which scorches the human heart and will by incinerating its sin, destroying its fear, and inflaming it to actively love God and neighbor (CXIX; p. 227). But she also puts forth innovative images of the Spirit that appear to be distinctive to her own theological and spiritual imagination. For example, she speaks of the Holy Spirit as "a mother who nurses [the soul] at the breast of divine charity" (CXLI; p. 292), and a tender waiter who serves the food of the Son on the table of the Father (LXXVIII; pp. 145-46).

Chan, Simon. *Spiritual Theology: A Systematic Study of the Christian Life.* Downers Grove, Ill.: InterVarsity, 1998.

After a brief methodological chapter explaining the character and goal of spiritual theology (focusing on the experience of spiritual growth), Chan argues that the foundation of Christian spirituality is the doctrine of God, which should be articulated in explicitly trinitarian terms. He argues that a spirituality that focuses only on the Father or only on the Son is inadequate, pointing to the need for these to be balanced by the "spirituality of the Spirit" represented in Pentecostal-charismatic churches. Chan does not spell out pneumatological doctrine in detail, but does pay special attention to the importance of the experience of the Spirit in theology.

Clayton, Philip. "In Whom We Have Our Being: Philosophical Resources for the Doctrine of the Spirit." In *Advents of the Spirit: An Introduction to the Current Study of Pneumatology,* edited by Bradford E. Hinze and D. Lyle Dabney. Milwaukee: Marquette University Press, 2001.

In this essay Clayton identifies what he sees as some of the most important philosophical shifts that impact the contemporary context within which constructive pneumatology must be done today. He suggests a "postfoundationalist" approach that rejects relativism but accepts a responsible pluralism, and calls for a pneumatology that moves beyond concepts of substance ontology, but does not give up on the possibility of metaphysics. Instead of beginning with "substance" as a foundational ontological principle, as did Spinoza and others, Clayton argues we should take advantage of the dynamism emphasized in the idealism that developed from Kant and Fichte through Hegel. Moving beyond such thinkers, however, Clayton commends a form of panentheism (the view that God is present throughout, but not limited to, creation) that attempts to link the idea of human spirit and infinite divine Spirit through a "personal" metaphysics. Recognizing (with Schleiermacher and Levinas) that human language cannot grasp the infinite, he nevertheless encourages systematic pneumatological reflection that makes sense of that limitation.

Coakley, Sarah. "'Femininity' and the Holy Spirit." In *Mirror to the Church: Reflections on Sexism,* edited by Monica Furlong. London: SPCK, 1988.

This essay is critical of Yves Congar's "question-begging" ascription of femininity to the Holy Spirit. In Congar's trinitarian thought the Spirit may be thought of as "mother who enables us to know our Father, God, and our brother, Jesus" (p. 124). While at first glance introducing a female third into the Trinity may seem like a welcome remedy to overused male imagery for God in Christian thought, Coakley argues that Congar's conception of the feminine Spirit as inherently comforting, gentle, and intimate poses the very real danger that "at worst, a 'feminine' Spirit may become nothing much more than the soothing but undervalued adjunct to the drama of an all-male household" (p. 132).

———. "Why Three? Some Further Reflections on the Origins of the Doctrine of the Trinity." In *Making and Remaking of Christian Doctrine.* Oxford: Clarendon Press, 1993.

In this essay Coakley deals with the issue of making sense of the Holy Spirit as a distinct hypostasis. After treating several contemporary theologians who have offered only partial answers to this question, she argues on the basis of Romans 8 that we ought to begin not with linear, rationalistic explanations, but rather with religious experiences of the Spirit and the Trinity in ecstatic prayer. Beginning with prayer allows us to conceive of the Holy Spirit as "a means of incorporation into the trinitarian life of God" (p. 36). In mystical prayer, we are brought into a "total experience of God [which] is here found to be ineluctably tri-faceted" (p. 37). She goes on to demonstrate that this experience-based approach was a persistent thread in early church doctrine and liturgy; however, experiential or mystical experiences of the Spirit were generally squelched or declared heretical in favor of more rational, sober approaches to doctrine. Why? Coakley suggests that there were political and sexual reasons. Namely, she surmises that second-century Montanist women, emboldened by God and speaking on behalf of Christ through the Spirit in an abandoned yet authoritative manner, were looked on as highly subversive by the early church. Coakley argues for the recovery of charismatic, mystical prayer in the Spirit as a powerful starting point for the articulation of trinitarian (and pneumatological) doctrine.

Coffey, David. "Spirit Christology and the Trinity." In *Advents of the Spirit: An Introduction to the Current Study of Pneumatology,* edited by Bradford E. Hinze and D. Lyle Dabney. Milwaukee: Marquette University Press, 2001.

Coffey is one of the most influential contemporary proponents of a revitalized Spirit-christology that emphasizes the Spirit's constitutive role in the Incarnation. The main point of such approaches is that christology has long been dominated by the concept of *Logos* to the exclusion of the role of the Spirit. But the biblical witness speaks not only of the Son sending the Spirit, but of the Spirit resting on, anointing, glorifying, and leading Jesus, and these aspects of the economy of salvation should be accounted for in christology. He finds resources for this task, surprisingly, in some lesser-known texts of Augustine and Cyril of Alexandria, who hint that the Incarnation can be understood as the Father's radical gift of the Holy Spirit to the humanity of Christ. Coffey's own proposal attempts to take seriously both "procession" and "return" models of the Trinity, which he believes can help reconcile Western "filioquism" and Eastern "monopatrism."

―――. "The Roman 'Clarification' of the Doctrine of the *Filioque.*" *International Journal of Systematic Theology* 5, no. 1 (2003).

In this essay Coffey exposits a 1995 Roman Catholic document on the *filioque* and engages some of the discussion that followed its publication. He contends that in the interest of ecumenical concerns, the document and its commentators have risked watering down the full content of the Western position on the *filioque,* which he sees as a "more developed, if excessively one-sided, position on the procession of the Holy Spirit." Coffey submits that "the ideal future ecumenical position on this subject must preserve the positive content of the Western achievement (jettisoning its one-sidedness), at the same time having as its central affirmation the great insight of the East, namely, the monarchy of the Father" (p. 12).

Comblin, José. *The Holy Spirit and Liberation.* Translated by Paul Burns. Maryknoll, N.Y.: Orbis Books, 1989.

This work is the first book-length treatment of pneumatology from the perspective of liberation theology. Critical of Western Christianity's "Christomonism," Comblin begins with experience — specifically, the experience of oppressed Latin American peoples — and emphasizes the active power of the Spirit who calls forth communities of freedom. Although he begins methodologically with the experience of the Spirit, Comblin also takes the reader through careful analyses of the biblical witness and relevant historical debates, interpreting them in light of a concern for the liberating power of the Spirit in concrete communities.

Come, Arnold B. *Human Spirit and Holy Spirit.* Philadelphia: Westminster, 1959.

Come argues that part of the problem with modern approaches to pneumatology is that they begin with abstract, metaphysical concepts of Spirit and then move toward making sense of the experience of the human spirit. He takes the opposite methodological approach, inspired by Søren Kierkegaard, of whose *Sickness Unto Death* he says: "two pages of one little book mark the watershed for the contemporary Christian view of man — perhaps for the whole of recent theology" (p. 32). Come intentionally devotes only one chapter explicitly to the Holy Spirit, and this after carefully attending to the relational dimensions of the experience of the human spirit in relation to God. Only in this way, he believes, can we overcome otherwise insoluble problems in Christian anthropology and pneumatology (such as dualism and individualism) that are based upon problematic metaphysical abstraction. Come concludes with a treatment of the "commonwealth of the Spirit," arguing that for Paul and Calvin, among others, life in the Spirit has to do with recognizing one's dependence on God and engaging in loving encounters with one's neighbors.

Congar, Yves. *I Believe in the Holy Spirit.* Translated by David Smith. Reprint edition, 3 vols. in 1. New York: Crossroad/Herder, 1997. First published as *Je crois en l'Esprit Saint,* 1979-80.

While many ideas are explored in Congar's influential three-volume work on the Holy Spirit, the overarching themes are the believer's life in the Spirit and the Spirit's role in making the church one. In the first volume, *The Experience of the Spirit,* Congar discusses the "experience and revelation of the Spirit" in the Old and New Testaments and in the history of Christianity. In the second volume, *Lord and Giver of Life,* he explores the ways that the Spirit brings unity to the church as the source of its diversity (catholicity) and continuity (apostolicity). This volume also addresses spiritual and anthropological issues; the Spirit is freedom, empowerment, and hope for believers as they are drawn into a direct filial relationship with the Father in Christ. In addition, it includes a discussion on the positive contribution of the charismatic renewal to the Catholic Church. The final volume, *The River of Life Flows in the East and in the West,* carefully analyzes the different historical views on the procession of the Spirit within the Trinity, and concludes that "trinitarian faith is the same in the East and in the West" (p. 213). Congar's treatment of the Spirit and the Trinity had important implications for the twentieth-century ecumenical movement. Alongside Burgess's trilogy (1984-1997), Congar's three volumes provide an excellent starting point for understanding the complexity of the development of the doctrine of the Holy Spirit.

Cooke, Bernard. *Power and the Spirit of God: Toward an Experience-Based Pneumatology.* New York: Oxford University Press, 2004.

This book explores pneumatology in light of the paradigm shift in the view of "power" that has emerged out of social scientific and literary critical analyses of human life (including the human relation to nature). Cooke suggests that developments in the late modern conceptualization of power represent one of the most significant challenges ever to face Christian theology. He emphasizes the eschatological and life-giving power of the Spirit. This does not mean that the power of the Spirit is apolitical, but that "divine Spirit-power works through nonviolent service. Instead of coercion, God's Spirit is an invitation to greater levels of life and happiness" (p. 185). Cooke employs the metaphor of "embrace" as a way of conceptualizing the Spirit's power of love, the divine "outreaching" in loving self-gift that invites the other into the freedom of friendship. His emphasis on experience, already indicated in the title, is another example of a growing tendency in late modern pneumatology toward integrating concerns about spiritual practices within the doctrine of the Spirit.

Dabney, D. Lyle. "Why Should the Last be First? The Priority of Pneumatology in Recent Theological Discussion." In *Advents of the Spirit: An Introduction to the Current Study of Pneumatology,* edited by Bradford E. Hinze and D. Lyle Dabney. Milwaukee: Marquette University Press, 2001.

In this essay Dabney notes the dramatic increase of theological attention to pneumatology in recent years, and explores the validity of the methodological claim that "talk of the s/Spirit should have priority in philosophical and/or theological discourse" (p. 240). Dabney explores this move in the work of philosopher Steven Smith and theologian Michael Welker, but the bulk of his essay is an outline of his own understanding of the ecclesial and cultural significance of "a theology of the third article." He believes that starting with pneumatology can help the Christian church connect to contemporary culture, after the dissolution of the link between Christendom and Western society. The "first article" theology of Roman Catholicism (focusing on the Father) and the "second article" theology of the Reformation (focusing on the Son) are no longer adequate for engaging the intellectual and social challenges to Christian theology today. Dabney proposes a "third article" theology that has the following characteristics: "It starts with the Spirit, it unfolds in the story of the Trinitarian mission of God in the world, and it finds its focus in the center of that story — In the life, death and resurrection of Jesus Christ" (p. 254).

Davis, Stephen T., Daniel Kendall, and Gerald O'Collins, eds. *The Trinity: An Interdisciplinary Symposium.* New York: Oxford, 1999.

This volume showcases several attempts to heal the division between strictly Eastern and Western approaches to the Trinity, most of which bear indirectly on questions of pneumatology. However, only the contribution of the charismatic New Testament scholar Gordon Fee deals with the Holy Spirit in any detail. Many of the other essays are characterized by attempts to defend the substance metaphysics used by Augustine and others, which not surprisingly leads them to focus on the way in which the substance of the Father and the substance of the Son are related. One of the values of the book is the diversity of voices, and readers will better understand how decisions in the doctrine of the Trinity ramify into treatments of the Holy Spirit.

Del Colle, Ralph. *Christ and the Spirit: Spirit-Christology in Trinitarian Perspective.* New York: Oxford University Press, 1994.

This book is the most comprehensive contemporary treatment of the historical development of Spirit-christology. Del Colle explores the emergence of pneumatological christology in the Orthodox tradition, with its imagery of the "two hands" of God. He also engages the Roman Catholic tradition, with special attention to neo-scholasticism and, more recently, the work of David Coffey. Along the way, he critically engages the pneumatological proposals of a variety of theologians, including Schleiermacher, Barth, Tillich, Lampe, Schoonberg, and several others. Del Colle's overall argument is that Spirit-christology is of crucial importance to the contemporary church, but that it must be grounded in a broader theology of grace in which there is a real relation between the divine persons and created reality, and the Holy Spirit is understood as having a proper and distinctive mission within the economy of salvation.

Dreyer, Elizabeth A. "An Advent of the Spirit: Medieval Mystics and Saints." In *Advents of the Spirit: An Introduction to the Current Study of Pneumatology,* edited by Bradford E. Hinze and D. Lyle Dabney. Milwaukee: Marquette University Press, 2001.

In this essay Dreyer surveys medieval theological and mystical accounts of the experience of the Holy Spirit in order to aid in the recovery of an appreciation of the important roles that Spirit-focused language, imagery, and symbols play in the spirituality of individuals, the life of the church, and academic theological arenas. She focuses on specific pneumatological themes in five authors: Augustine ("The Spirit and the Power of Speech"), Hildegard of Bingen ("The 'Greening' of the Spirit"), Bernard of Clairvaux ("The Spirit as Kiss of the Beloved"), Bonaventure ("The Spirit as Magnanimous God"), and Catherine of Siena ("The Spirit as Servant").

Dunn, James D. G. "Towards the Spirit of Christ: The Emergence of the Distinctive Features of Christian Pneumatology." In *The Work of the Spirit: Pneumatology and Pentecostalism,* edited by Michael Welker. Grand Rapids: Eerdmans, 2006.

Dunn argues that the concept *ruach* was an "existential" term from the beginning, referring to an experience of an awesome and mysterious power. He suggests that in pre-Christian Judaism, there appears to have been no anticipation that a messianic figure would also be a bestower of the Spirit. John the Baptist seems to have been the first to use the image of an eschatological redeemer who would baptize in the Spirit. The early church came to view the exalted Christ as the one who pours out the Spirit (Acts 2:33-36). For Dunn the explosive force of Christianity's distinctiveness is connected to the perception of a transition in Jesus' own relation to the Spirit of God, namely, from one who had been inspired and anointed by the Spirit to the one who dispenses the Spirit. Dunn argues that it was an ecstatic experience of the phenomena of the Spirit that empowered believers and fueled the mission of the church. He suggests that academic theology must learn to be unembarrassed by the fact that Christianity began as an enthusiastic sect, which has much in common with twentieth-century Pentecostalism. At the same time, he encourages contemporary charismatic communities to recognize the importance of "discerning the spirits," a task that may be facilitated by theological reflection.

Edwards, Denis. *Breath of Life: A Theology of the Creator Spirit.* Maryknoll, N.Y.: Orbis, 2004.

Edwards outlines a pneumatology that engages the whole evolutionary history of the universe, appropriating Basil of Caesarea in order to depict the Spirit as the breath of God, the communion-bringer, who breathes life into a universe of creatures and enfolds human beings in grace.

Edwards, Jonathan. *The Miscellanies.* In *The Works of Jonathan Edwards,* edited by Thomas A. Schafer. New Haven: Yale University Press, 1994.

The emphasis on beauty and dynamism in many of Edwards's philosophical writings has come to the fore in recent scholarship, leading several theologians to retrieve this dimension of his authorship for articulating the doctrine of the Trinity, indirectly shaping contemporary discourse on pneumatology.

————. "An Essay on the Trinity." In *Treatise on Grace and Other Posthumously Published Writings,* edited by Paul Helm. Cambridge: James Clarke, 1971.

This is one of the many explicitly trinitarian works of Edwards that are getting increased attention among Reformed theologians.

Engberg-Pedersen, Troels. *Paul and the Stoics.* Louisville: Westminster John Knox, 2000.

This book offers an interpretation of Paul's view of transformation that engages the scholarship on Stoicism that has emerged during the last thirty years. Engberg-Pedersen demonstrates how Paul appropriates but also moves beyond the Stoic emphasis on the way in which an individual is transformed through belonging to a larger group. For both Paul and the Stoics, albeit in different ways, *pneuma* is that which brings about the transformation.

Eusebius. *Church History*. Translated by Arthur Cushman McGiffert. NPNF2, vol. 1. Peabody, Mass.: Hendrickson, 1994.

Eusebius of Caesarea (260-339) was the court theologian of the Emperor Constantine, and is widely regarded as the first major Christian historian. A champion of unity in the empire and order in the church, he was a harsh critic of Montanism because it appeared to threaten both governmental and ecclesial authority. Referencing an anonymous critic, he writes that the leaders of the "New Prophecy" — Montanus, Priscilla, and Maximilla — were inspired not by the Holy Spirit but rather by "the arrogant spirit [which] taught them to revile the entire universal Church under heaven, because the spirit of false prophecy received neither honor from it nor entrance into it" (V.16.9; p. 232). Eusebius contributed to the church's gradual movement toward a greater emphasis on hierarchy, orderliness, the authority of bishops, and collusion with the power of the Roman Empire, and the concurrent movement away from ecstatic expressions (gifts or *charismata*) of the Holy Spirit as the basis for the church's identity.

Fee, Gordon D. *God's Empowering Presence: The Holy Spirit in the Letters of Paul*. Peabody, Mass.: Hendrickson, 1994.

This is one of the most comprehensive treatments of the Pauline understanding of the Spirit of God by a New Testament scholar. Fee begins with an introduction to the theme and outlines some of the key distinctions among Greek terms relevant to pneumatology. He divides the rest of the book into two parts. In Part I ("Analysis"), Fee exegetes each of the significant passages that use the idea of the Spirit in the Pauline corpus, from the Thessalonian correspondence to the Pastoral Epistles. Part II ("Synthesis") draws together his findings around several key themes, such as eschatological fulfillment, personal presence, and the relation of the Spirit to salvation and the church. The final chapter summarizes the distinctives of Pauline pneumatology, contrasts them with the marginalization of the Spirit in so much contemporary theology, and calls for a renewed emphasis on the Spirit as central not only to Christian doctrine but to the experienced life of the believer and the believing community.

Ganoczy, Alexandre. "Word and Spirit in the Catholic Tradition." In *Conflicts About the Holy Spirit*, edited by Hans Küng and Jürgen Moltmann. New York: Seabury Press, 1979.

This essay compares and contrasts the pneumatologies of John Calvin and the Council of Trent, suggesting that Vatican II offers new opportunities for integrating the concerns of both.

Gebara, Ivone. "Option for the Poor as an Option for Poor Women." In *The Power of Naming: A Concilium Reader in Feminist Liberation Theology,* edited by Elisabeth Schüssler Fiorenza. Maryknoll, N.Y.: Orbis, 1996.

In this short essay Brazilian feminist theologian Ivone Gebara discusses what the gospel of liberation means for poor Latin American women. She argues that poor women must be empowered to opt for themselves, to opt for others, and to opt for "a new future of justice and love" (p. 148). This work is important for pneumatology because Gebara is clear that the Spirit is integral to the process of women's empowerment to freely choose for themselves, others, and a hopeful future: "By a significant number of women God is no longer seen in the image of a man, father, husband, or son, but as Spirit, breath of life, energy refusing to be locked in a box. . . . The power called freedom for many women is like being pregnant with the Spirit" (p. 147).

Gregory of Nazianzus. *Select Orations.* Translated by Charles Gordon Browne and James Edward Swallow. NPNF2, vol. 7. Peabody, Mass.: Hendrickson, 1994.

In his fifth theological oration, "On the Holy Spirit," Gregory explicitly defends the claim that the Spirit is God (X; p. 321). He also suggests the idea that the historical revelation of the Trinity is progressive: "The Old Testament proclaimed the Father openly, and the Son more obscurely. The New manifested the Son, and suggested the Deity of the Spirit. Now the Spirit Himself dwells among us, and supplies us with a clearer demonstration of Himself" (XXVI; p. 326). Other important sermons for his doctrine of the Spirit are "The Oration on Pentecost," "Oration on the Holy Lights," and the "Oration on Baptism."

Gregory of Nyssa. *On the Holy Spirit.* Translated by William Moore and Henry Austin Wilson. NPNF2, vol. 5. Peabody, Mass.: Hendrickson, 1994.

Only a fragment of this treatise remains, but what has survived provides a good synopsis of Gregory's pneumatology. He builds upon the arguments of his older brother, Basil, to defend the deity of the Spirit against the attacks of the *Pneumatomachoi.* Integrating neo-Platonic metaphysical concepts with rich, poetic imagery, this treatise emphasizes the Spirit's infinite perfection and goodness. Gregory elaborates on the intimate reciprocal glorification of the Spirit with the Father and the Son, and states that it is the Spirit who extends this glory to us so that we can be deified. He argues that denial of the Spirit's full divinity is a denial of Christianity altogether; furthermore, to despise and misunderstand the Holy Spirit is to despise and misunderstand oneself, since the Spirit is the Giver of all Life.

————. *On the Holy Trinity, and of the Godhead of the Holy Spirit.* Translated by William Moore and Henry Austin Wilson. NPNF2, vol. 5. Peabody, Mass: Hendrickson, 1994.

In this short letter to Eusthathius, Gregory defends against the accusation of tritheism. He seeks to demonstrate the Spirit's divinity by arguing that since the Spirit has an "inseparable association" with Father and Son in regard to the divine attributes (such as wisdom, righteousness, and life-giving power), it is clear that the Spirit cannot be excluded from the "community" of the Godhead.

Gregory of Palamas. *The Triads.* Edited with an introduction by John Meyendorff. Translated by N. Gendle. New York: Paulist, 1983.

This is a classic statement of the Eastern doctrine of the divine energies, including the deifying energies of the Spirit, which is the basis for the understanding of salvation as *theosis.* In Part I we discuss his role in the Eastern Orthodox tradition and its resistance to the *filioque.*

Groppe, Elizabeth Teresa. *Yves Congar's Theology of the Holy Spirit.* New York: Oxford University Press, 2004.

Commending the distinctive contribution of Congar to contemporary Roman Catholic theology, Groppe applauds his integration of anthropology, ecclesiology, and pneumatology, arguing that this opens up new space for ecumenical dialogue. She points out that Congar's immediate Roman Catholic theological predecessors often separated an anthropological theology of the Spirit's indwelling of individual persons from a systematic theology of the Spirit's presence in the church. But she submits that Congar's integration of these themes can transform a number of key questions in Catholic theology. The question of whether the Catholic Church should be a hierarchy or a democracy can be reframed in a way that emphasizes that the Spirit is common to all and the church has its origins in God. The question of the relation between "individual and church" can be reframed in a way that emphasizes the concept of "persons in communion." Finally, the question of whether "the indwelling of the Spirit in the just soul is proper to the Spirit or simply appropriated" (p. 163) can be reframed in a way that emphasizes the Spirit's indwelling of interpersonal and ecclesial relationships.

Guyon, Madame Jeanne-Marie. *A Short and Easy Method of Prayer.* Napa, Calif.: Lulu Press, 2005.

Madame Guyon (1648-1717) was a French Catholic mystic who was persecuted for her insistence on the necessity of radical passivity in relation to God. She was a leader in the Quietist movement, which taught that through utter abandonment in mystical prayer, an individual soul may pass beyond sin and achieve full union with God. In this book, her most well-known work, Guyon insists that all are called to the "prayer of the heart" (as opposed to the "prayer of the head"). She discourages set forms of prayer that are based on memory and repetition, and instead advocates reliance on the leadings of the Holy Spirit, who intercedes for us and "indites" our prayers and petitions. The Roman Catholic Church condemned Guyon's passive spirituality as heretical, and she was imprisoned from 1695-1703.

Hegel, G. W. F. *Phenomenology of Spirit.* Translated by A. V. Miller. New York: Oxford University Press, 1977.

This book was one of the most important philosophical works of the early nineteenth century and exerted considerable influence on (and provoked considerable antagonism toward) Christian pneumatology. For Hegel, "Spirit" *(Geist)* develops itself and explicates itself through a series of dialectical movements, from consciousness through self-consciousness, reason, Spirit, religion, and absolute knowing. The simple content of the "absolute religion" is "the incarnation of the divine Being, or the fact that it essentially and directly has the shape of self-consciousness . . . In this religion the divine Being is known as Spirit, or this religion is the consciousness of the divine Being that is Spirit. For Spirit is the knowledge of one's self in the externalization of oneself; the being that is the movement of retaining its self-identity in its otherness" (p. 459).

―――. *Lectures on the Philosophy of Religion.* Edited by Peter C. Hodgson. 3 vols. Berkeley: University of California Press, 1987.

In these lectures Hegel treats the "consummate religion" in which self-consciousness becomes object to itself. He speaks of three "elements," which are not external distinctions but "the activity, the developed vitality, of absolute spirit itself" (vol. 3, p. 274). The first element is the idea of God in and for itself, the second is representation (appearance), and the third is community (spirit). Many theologians have worried that Hegel's way of formulating the doctrine of the Trinity and linking it to Spirit is simply a projection of idealist reflection logic onto God as a single subject. Another concern is that his formulation collapses into panentheism (at best) or pantheism (at worst). This emphasis on immanence was countered among many later Christian theologians who stressed the transcendence of the Spirit; this tension continues to characterize much of the current pneumatological debate.

Hendry, George S. *The Holy Spirit in Christian Theology.* Philadelphia: Westminster, 1956.

This book does not offer a systematic presentation of the doctrine of the Holy Spirit, but attempts to show how many of the core problems of modern theology are connected to their pneumatological assumptions and implications. He notes that the relative lack of attention to the person of the Spirit in the tradition is in part due to the inherent ambiguity of the very idea of "Spirit," as well as to the diversity in the biblical witness to the Spirit of God. Hendry limits himself to an exploration of five problems, comprising the five chapters of the book. First, what is the relation between the Spirit and the man Jesus Christ? Second, how is the Spirit related to the other persons of the trinitarian God? Third, how is the Holy Spirit related to the church? Fourth, related especially to the Protestant (especially Reformed) answer to the third question, is the issue of the relation of the Spirit and the Word. Finally, he examines the question of the relation between the Holy Spirit and the human spirit.

Heppe, Heinrich. *Reformed Dogmatics: Set out and Illustrated from the Sources.* Revised and edited by E. Bizer. Translated by G. T. Thomson. London: Allen & Unwin, 1950.

The most readily available English source for quotations on the Holy Spirit from the Reformed Scholastics from the late sixteenth to early eighteenth centuries.

Heron, Alasdair. *The Holy Spirit: The Holy Spirit in the Bible, the History of Christian Thought, and Recent Theology.* Philadelphia: Westminster, 1983.

As the subtitle suggests, Heron's book is an overview of the understanding of the Spirit throughout the Christian tradition. Part I examines the concept of the Spirit in Scripture, tracing the various meanings of the *ruach* of Yahweh in Israel's experience. He gives an overview of the role of the Dead Sea Scrolls and the wisdom tradition "between the Testaments" and then outlines the link between the Spirit of God and the Spirit of Christ in the New Testament. Part II identifies "patterns in pneumatology." Heron outlines the "first sketches" in the second and third centuries after Christ and then explores the doctrinal discussions of the Spirit as Lord, Life-giver, God's Love, God's Gift, and the problematic "soul of the church." He also traces the emphasis on the Spirit as Enlightener and Sanctifier in the early modern period. Part III is a survey of current issues, including the challenge of Pentecostalism; the relation between spirit, self, and world in human experience; and the twentieth-century debates over the Third Person of the Trinity.

Hilberath, Bernd Jochen. "Identity through Self-Transcendence: The Holy Spirit and the Fellowship of Free Persons." In *Advents of the Spirit: An Introduction to the Current Study of Pneumatology,* edited by Bradford E. Hinze and D. Lyle Dabney. Milwaukee: Marquette University Press, 2001.

This essay explicitly attempts to link the way in which human persons become free in fellowship with others to an understanding of the free relations between the Father and the Son in the trinitarian life. Hilberath begins by arguing that an often missed reason for the deficit in treatments of the Holy Spirit is a spiritual one, namely, the failure to recognize that "the experience that self-transcendence toward others does not mean loss of one's own identity, but rather furthers it or makes it possible." His thesis is that the Holy Spirit reveals what it means to acquire and preserve one's identity, "coming to oneself by giving room to the other" (p. 267). Supporting his thesis by appealing to Scripture and appropriating some Rahnerian themes, Hilberath concludes that we should think of person and relation as belonging essentially together, a fact that is disclosed in the idea of the Holy Spirit as "the event of loving encounter, the space into which Father and Son transcend themselves," as the one who binds them in love into unity (p. 282). The Holy Spirit is the model of personhood insofar as he is both with himself and allowing the Father and the Son to be with themselves in the other. The essay concludes with some implications of his proposal for ecclesiology, and specific criteria for discerning the new life together in the Spirit.

Hildegard of Bingen. *Scivias.* Translated by Mother Columba Hart and Jane Bishop. New York: Paulist Press, 1990.

Hildegard was a medieval German mystic. She experienced and understood the Holy Spirit as empowering her to speak out prophetically against political and ecclesial corruption. Hildegard's pneumatology in *Scivias* is marked by vibrant, natural imagery; she depicts the Holy Spirit as "eager freshness" (III.7.9; p. 418), a "torrent" (II.4.2; p. 190), a "gentle animal" (II.3.32; p. 182), and a "flame" (II.4.1; p. 190).

Hinze, Bradford E. "Releasing the Power of the Spirit in a Trinitarian Ecclesiology." In *Advents of the Spirit: An Introduction to the Current Study of Pneumatology,* edited by Bradford E. Hinze and D. Lyle Dabney. Milwaukee: Marquette University Press, 2001.

This essay is an attempt to demonstrate the historical contribution of several Roman Catholic theologians to the task of linking the doctrine of the Holy Spirit to a relational ecclesiology. Hinze begins with Johann Adam Möhler's Spirit-centered ecclesiology in the middle of the nineteenth century. The bulk of his chapter, however, attends to the contributions of key twentieth-century Catholic theologians. He summarizes the work of such as Yves Congar, Heribert Mühlen, and Karl Rahner, surrounding and following the Second Vatican Council. Leonardo Boff and Edward Schillebeeckx are offered as examples of the way in which those interested in social advocacy have been pioneers in pneumatology. Hinze also appreciates the work of theologians like Henri de Lubac, Hans Urs von Balthasar, and Joseph Ratzinger (now Pope Benedict XVI), who warned against "excessive pneumaticism." He concludes with his own call for a trinitarian ecclesiology that can "release and receive" the full power of the Spirit, understood as the "co-institutor" of the church.

Hodge, Charles. *Systematic Theology.* 3 vols. Grand Rapids: Eerdmans, 1981.

Originally published 1871-1873, this is a comprehensive presentation of Christian doctrine by one of the most important religious figures in nineteenth-century American history. He reacted strongly against Schleiermacher's approach to the Holy Spirit and reiterated many of the seventeenth-century Protestant Scholastic formulations of the doctrine.

Hollenweger, Walter J. *Pentecostalism: Origins and Developments Worldwide.* Peabody, Mass.: Hendrickson, 1997.

Building on *The Pentecostals* (1972), this book outlines a variety of Pentecostal theologies from around the world, using the framework of the five historical "roots" of the movement: Black oral, Catholic, evangelical, critical, and ecumenical. He concludes with a discussion of the problem of "ex-Pentecostals" — persons who have been hurt by the movement — and highlights the promise that Pentecostal spirituality holds for future ecumenical dialogue.

————. *The Pentecostals: The Charismatic Movement in the Churches.* Translated by R. A. Wilson. Minneapolis: Augsburg, 1972.

This comprehensive and ecumenically-sensitive study is widely regarded as a classic resource for understanding the complexity of the history and diversity within the theologies of the global Pentecostal movement. Of particular interest for students of pneumatology is Hollenweger's chapter on the Pentecostal doctrine of the Spirit (pp. 321-52), wherein he treats the topics of inspiration, salvation, sanctification, the baptism of the Holy Spirit, speaking in tongues, and prophecy.

Hollingsworth, Andrea. "Spirit and Voice: Toward a Feminist Pentecostal Pneumatology." *Pneuma: The Journal for the Society of Pentecostal Studies* 29, no. 2 (2007): 189-213.

This article suggests that greater attention to Pentecostal spirituality in feminist pneumatology may provide new ways to link women's empowerment with the doctrine of the Holy Spirit. After an overview of feminist pneumatology and Pentecostal spirituality, it offers an exposition of the pneumatological writings of Anglican theologian Sarah Coakley, arguing that her insights lead us to ask about the ways in which charismatic piety might contribute to the liberation and empowerment of Pentecostal women in the Majority World today. Some spiritual and social aspects of the experiences of contemporary Pentecostal Latinas are then explored. Here the essay discusses the problematic dynamics of patriarchal attitudes and complicity with globalization that are associated with Pentecostalism in Latin America, but also highlights sociological research which shows that Latin American women's ecstatic experiences of the Spirit are frequently linked with an increased sense of personal subjectivity, and the ability to "give voice" in both public and private spheres. The article concludes with a proposal for speaking of the Holy Spirit as the divine voice, suggesting that this may be one way to move toward a constructive feminist Pentecostal pneumatology.

Humphrey, Edith M. *Ecstasy and Intimacy: When the Holy Spirit Meets the Human Spirit.* Grand Rapids: Eerdmans, 2006.

Humphrey's book demonstrates the growing trend to more closely link pneumatology with spirituality. For her, "Christian spirituality is the study and experience of what happens when the Holy Spirit meets the human spirit" (p. 31). Humphrey guides readers through the writings of many Christian mystics and theologians, always with the overarching goal of countering popular notions of spirituality that are divorced from key Christian doctrines (Incarnation, Trinity, and pneumatology in particular). Part prayerbook, part theology text, Humphrey's work is geared toward an educated lay audience. It includes many poems, prayers, and hymn lyrics, which are designed to encourage the reader to integrate meditation with study. It also sets forth questions for further reflection and dialogue at the close of chapters for those who may be reading and discussing it in a group setting.

Ignatius of Loyola. "Selections from the Spiritual Diary." In *Ignatius of Loyola: Spiritual Exercises and Selected Works,* translated by Edward J. Malatesta and George E. Ganss; edited by George E. Ganss. New York: Paulist Press, 1991.

Ignatius's diary consists mostly of prayers and accounts of spiritual experiences. It contains many sensual references to the Holy Spirit; for example, he describes an experience of "speaking with" the Spirit, and then, through tears, seeming "to see him or perceive him in dense brightness or in the color of a flame of fire burning in an unusual way" (I.1.14; p. 241).

―――――. "The Spiritual Exercises." In *Ignatius of Loyola: Spiritual Exercises and Selected Works,* translated and edited by George E. Ganss. New York: Paulist Press, 1991.

This manual of prayer and confession is by far Ignatius's most influential work. It has been the defining element of Jesuit spirituality for over four hundred years, and today is a source of renewal for countless spiritual seekers — many of them non-Catholic. Through repentance and confession, the exercitant is transformed and led into an increasing desire to serve in the way of Jesus Christ, and be led of the Spirit.

Irenaeus of Lyons. *Against Heresies.* ANF, vol. 1. Peabody, Mass.: Hendrickson, 1994.

The classic text in which Irenaeus develops the imagery of the Son and the Spirit as the "two hands of God."

Jenson, Robert. *Systematic Theology.* 2 vols. Grand Rapids: Eerdmans, 1997, 1999.

This is a comprehensive treatment of Christian doctrine by one of the leading Lutheran theologians of our time. Jenson's belief that "Pentecost is a peer of Easter" leads him to develop a pneumatology that is as robust as his christology.

―――――. "What is the Point of Trinitarian Theology?" In *Trinitarian Theology Today,* edited by Christoph Schwöbel. Edinburgh: T&T Clark, 1995.

Jenson deals with the particularity of the personhood of the Spirit within the context of this chapter on the broader theme of the Trinity.

John of the Cross. *John of the Cross: Selected Writings*. Translated and edited by Kieran Kavanaugh. New York: Paulist Press, 1987.

> "The Living Flame of Love" is a poem (and commentary) composed to depict how a soul comes to complete union with Father, Son, and Holy Spirit. John writes of the Spirit as the fire in which the soul is "consumed and transformed." The Spirit is the vibrant flame that "flares up" within the burning soul of the person that is being united to God (I.3; p. 295). The "Dark Night of the Soul" is not explicitly focused on pneumatology, but it is essential for understanding John's view of the experience of the Spirit. The "Spiritual Canticle" is a poem based on the Song of Songs, which demonstrates John's allegorical pneumatology.

John of Damascus. *Exposition of the Orthodox Faith*. NPNF2, vol. 9. Peabody, Mass.: Hendrickson, 1994.

> This is a summary of the theology of the patristic fathers, especially the Cappadocians, which clearly sets out the basic elements of their pneumatology.

Johnson, Elizabeth A. *Friends of God and Prophets: A Feminist Theological Reading of the Communion of Saints*. New York: Continuum, 1998.

> In this book, Catholic feminist theologian Elizabeth A. Johnson explores the topic of the communion of saints, which is, in her words, "the whole community of people graced by the Spirit of God" (p. 1). In Chapter 11, Johnson argues that the Spirit's action points toward an eternal future for persons beyond death, and describes three actions of the Spirit that lead to this hope: (1) creation (the Spirit is the matrix for all reality, and life after death coheres with a view of the Creator Spirit as that which guides the community into ever-more complex forms of consciousness); (2) resurrection (the Spirit gives all things hope for resurrection — humans, earth, cosmos); and (3) self-communication in grace (in death, the Spirit brings us simultaneously closer to God, and more alive to self). In Johnson's panentheistic pneumatology, the Spirit brings all things together in redemptive relation, and this fellowship is at the core of the symbol of the communion of saints. This chapter offers fruitful theological material for linking pneumatology with ecclesiology and eschatology.

————. *She Who Is: The Mystery of God in Feminist Theological Discourse*. New York: Crossroad, 1992. Page references are to the tenth anniversary edition (2005).

> In this book, Johnson re-imagines the Trinity by employing the feminine symbol of Sophia (Wisdom) to describe each of the divine persons. Spirit-

Sophia is the creative, renewing, empowering, gracing presence of the mystery of God in the economy of redemption who brings us into solidarity with others (particularly those who are suffering). Johnson emphasizes that in Sophia's dynamic "inner relatedness" there is no subordination.

————. *Women, Earth, and Creator Spirit.* New York: Paulist, 1993.

Here Johnson offers an ecofeminist approach to pneumatology. She situates her argument in concerns over the exploitation of the earth and the marginalization of women (which she sees as closely related phenomena), and proposes a "theology of the Creator Spirit [which] overcomes the dualism of spirit and matter with all of its ramifications, and leads to the realization of the sacredness of the earth" (pp. 59-60).

Justin Martyr. *First Apology* and *Dialogue with Trypho.* ANF, vol. 1. Peabody, Mass.: Hendrickson, 1994.

Justin (100-165 A.D.) was among the most influential of the early apologists. During this period theologians tended to focus more on the *Logos* than the *Pneuma* and this is reflected in Justin's pneumatology.

Kärkkäinen, Veli-Matti. *Pneumatology: The Holy Spirit in Ecumenical, International, and Contextual Perspective.* Grand Rapids: Baker Academic, 2002.

This book by a leading contemporary Pentecostal theologian engaged in ecumenical dialogue provides a helpful introductory overview to the state of pneumatology at the turn of the millennium. Kärkkäinen covers biblical and historical issues in the development of the doctrine of the Holy Spirit, and connects the recent surge of interest in pneumatology to developments in ecumenical dialogue following the Second Vatican Council of the Roman Catholic Church, the rapid growth of Pentecostal and charismatic Christianity, and the contributions of feminist, ecological, and liberation theologians.

————. *Toward a Pneumatological Theology: Pentecostal and Ecumenical Perspectives on Ecclesiology, Soteriology, and Theology of Mission.* Edited by Amos Yong. Lanham, Md.: University Press of America, 2002.

In this collection of essays, Kärkkäinen treats topics related to church, salvation, and evangelization, all with the goal of charting a course "toward" a pneumatological theology, which is defined as "a theology informed by and founded on the Spirit of the Triune God" (p. vii). He frequently comes back to certain themes in this work: Trinity, communion, cultural issues, and social justice. It is significant because it is a good example of scholarship coming from the emerging contemporary domain of Pentecostal pneumatology — a domain which (generally speaking) seeks to speak of the Spirit in ecumenically sensitive, culturally aware, and robustly trinitarian ways.

―――. "How to Speak of the Spirit among Religions." In *The Work of the Spirit: Pneumatology and Pentecostalism,* edited by Michael Welker. Grand Rapids: Eerdmans, 2006.

Kärkkäinen argues that the dynamic communion and alterity that is the divine life of Father, Son, and Spirit should function as the methodological ground for speaking of the Spirit in the context of dialogue with the world's religions.

Kim, Kirsteen. *The Holy Spirit in the World: A Global Conversation.* Maryknoll, N.Y.: Orbis, 2007.

Kim's book is bracketed by a treatment of two conferences sponsored by the World Council of Churches that aimed to facilitate dialogue on the doctrine of the Holy Spirit. The introduction focuses on the pneumatological controversy in Canberra in 1991 and the epilogue reviews the conference on missions and ecumenism in Athens in 2005, whose theme was "Come, Holy Spirit, heal and reconcile." This is the global and pragmatic context within which Kim provides a clear overview of some of the most significant pneumatological contributions in the intervening years. After briefly summarizing the "postmodern" setting that has provided a new context for interpreting the biblical witness to the Spirit (chapters 1 and 2), the book turns to a treament of a variety of different types of pneumatologies. The twentieth-century West has tended to emphasize the "Spirit of Mission" using terms like "impulse," "guidance," and "power" (chapter 3). The Eastern Orthodox churches have emphasized terms like "unity," "creation," and "history" in their understanding of the "mission of the Spirit" (chapter 4). The fifth chapter reviews several dimensions of some Indian theologian's understanding of "mission in the Spirit," including an emphasis on dialogue, inculturation, and liberation. The sixth chapter offers a similar review of Korean pneumatologies that stress "mission among the Spirits," using terms like "release," "blessing," and "harmony." The final major chapter deals with the difficult question of the discernment among spirits and spiritualities in developing a theology of the Holy Spirit in a plural world.

Kinkel, Gary Steven. *Our Dear Mother the Spirit: An Investigation of Count Zinzendorf's Theology and Praxis.* Lanham, Md.: University Press of America, 1990.

Kinkel explores the pneumatology of eighteenth-century Pietist Count Ludwig von Zinzendorf, the founder of the Moravian Church. He focuses his discussion on Zinzendorf's use of the term "Mother" to describe the Spirit. First, he argues that Zinzendorf viewed the Holy Spirit as the agent who created and guided the people of Herrnhut (the first Moravian community). Second, he posits that Zinzendorf spoke of the Spirit as "Mother" because he wanted to communicate to the people of Herrnhut a "concrete picture and feeling of what the Christian Scriptures said the Holy Spirit does. This way of talking was supposed to move hearts without losing theological content" (p. 222). Third, Kinkel suggests that Zinzendorf's pneumatology was an outgrowth of Luther's pneumatology, and that Zinzendorf rejected subordinationism and hierarchy in the Trinity as well as in the Christian community. Practically speaking, this means that at Herrnhut, "women were to participate in the administration of the Christian community and the accomplishment of its mission on a level absolutely equal to that of males" (pp. 223-24). Kinkel's book is an important resource for understanding Pietist pneumatology and spirituality, which grew out of a reaction against the rational approaches of Protestant scholasticism and instead sought to emphasize themes such as warmth, intimacy, and community.

Küng, Hans, and Jürgen Moltmann, eds. *Conflicts about the Holy Spirit*. New York: Seabury, 1979.

Although the essays in this edited volume are relatively short, they provide a good introduction to key pneumatological themes, such as the relation between the Son and the Spirit *(filioque)*, between the Word and the Spirit (the Reformation), between the Spirit and Office (the question of Rome), and between Spirit and spirits (the question of the charismatic movement), with contributions from a broad range of traditions.

LaCugna, Catherine Mowry. *God for Us: The Trinity and Christian Life*. New York: HarperCollins, 1992.

LaCugna argues that soteriology and trinitarian theology are inseparable, and that "The ultimate source of all reality is not a 'by-itself' or an 'in-itself' but a person, a toward-another" (p. 14). She defines pneumatology as the "theology of divine ecstasy" (p. 355) and speaks of the Holy Spirit as the "freedom of God" who "brings the creature into union and communion with God and other creatures" (p. 298).

―――. "God in Communion with Us." In *Freeing Theology: The Essentials of Theology in Feminist Perspective*, edited by Catherine Mowry LaCugna. New York: HarperCollins, 1993.

Concisely and understandably, LaCugna traces the historical development of orthodox trinitarian doctrine, exposes hierarchical "complementarian" notions of the Trinity, and reviews attempts made at addressing and correcting these. She is critical of approaches that depict the Holy Spirit as the "female person" in God; in her view, this only solidifies gender stereotypes and presents God as two-thirds male. She concludes by offering her own correction, which consists of a retrieval of the themes of equality, communion, and personhood in the Trinity, and a call to gender-inclusive language for God.

Lampe, Geoffrey. *God as Spirit.* Oxford: Clarendon Press, 1977.

This book is often held up as an example of a dominant modalist tendency in Western theology. Lampe's title is to be taken literally; we are to understand God as Spirit, and this refers to the one God who is immanently present to all of creation, who acts in the Christ event, and who works interactively in and with the human spirit — especially in the church. Such an approach virtually dissolves the *filioque* debate, which Lampe observes is a "controversy about nothing real" (p. 226).

Lossky, Vladimir. *In the Image and Likeness of God.* Crestwood, N.Y.: St. Vladimir's Seminary Press, 1985.

In this book Lossky demonstrates the significance of the concept of *imago Dei* for the whole of Eastern Orthodox theology. "The Procession of the Holy Spirit" (Chapter 4) describes the unique features of Orthodox pneumatology, and outlines the development of the doctrine in the context of the Eastern distinction between essence and energies, as well as a trinitarian understanding of *theosis.*

————. *The Mystical Theology of the Eastern Church.* Crestwood, N.Y.: St. Vladimir's Seminary Press, 1998.

This work serves as a resource for understanding the pneumatological contributions of this leading Orthodox theologian to the ecumenical dialogue between East and West in the twentieth century. Of particular relevance is Chapter 8, "The Economy of the Holy Spirit."

Luther, Martin. *Smaller Catechism.* In *The Book of Concord,* translated and edited by Theodore Tapper. Philadelphia: Muhlenberg Press, 1959.

In the twentieth century, Luther scholars have increasingly recognized the centrality of the doctrine of the Holy Spirit for this influential Reformer. The *Smaller Catechism* is one of the places where Luther describes the work of the Holy Spirit in the process of salvation.

————. *Bondage of the Will.* Translated by J. I. Packer and O. R. Johnston. Grand Rapids: Baker, 2003.

This polemical treatise does not treat the Holy Spirit in great detail, but does illustrate Luther's use of the ideas of divine will and power, as well as personhood.

Macchia, Frank. "The Kingdom and the Power: Spirit Baptism in Pentecostal and Ecumenical Perspective." In *The Work of the Spirit: Pneumatology and Pentecostalism,* edited by Michael Welker. Grand Rapids: Eerdmans, 2006.

Here Pentecostal theologian Frank Macchia draws on the experience of Spirit baptism to articulate an ecumenical pneumatology. He points out that Reformed/evangelical, sacramental, and Holiness/Pentecostal traditions have generally defined the "baptism of the Holy Spirit" quite differently — usually in ways specific to the unique ecclesiological concerns of those particular traditions. But in Macchia's view a bigger question needs to be asked — a question that is relevant for all Christians, namely, how is Spirit baptism related to the arrived and arriving kingdom of God? Macchia's suggested answer is that the baptism of the Holy Spirit is ultimately about the church participating in the final sanctification of creation. For him, a dual emphasis on the eschatological and participative aspects of Spirit baptism can provide room for pneumatological and spiritual commonality among varying traditions at the same time that it upholds and values their "emerging and diverse experiences of the Spirit" (p. 125).

MacRobert, Iain. "The Black Roots of Pentecostalism." In *African American Religion: Interpretive Essays in History and Culture,* edited by Timothy E. Fulop and Albert J. Raboteau. New York: Routledge, 1997.

This provocative essay explores Pentecostalism's historic origins in black North American Christianity, and exposes the racism that has contributed to the failure of many white Pentecostal preachers, historians, and theologians to recognize "the crucial influences of African American Christianity" (p. 297) on Pentecostalism. MacRobert points out that in the literature, white contributors to the movement such as Charles Fox Parham have often been eulogized while black leaders like William J. Seymour have often been marginalized. He urges white Pentecostals to acknowledge that their experience of the Holy Spirit has deep roots in the religion of the African Diaspora — a "syncretism of West African primal religion and culture with Western Christianity in the crucible of New World slavery" (p. 299). He argues that white Pentecostals in the United States have intentionally dissociated themselves from their black roots and have sought to "purge [Pentecostalism] of its more obviously black and radical elements which, however, re-emerge again and again wherever Pentecostals of the African Diaspora meet for worship" (p. 305).

Maddox, Randy L. *Responsible Grace: John Wesley's Practical Theology*. Nashville: Abingdon, 1994.

This overview of Wesley's theology contains a chapter on "Holy Spirit — The Presence of Responsible Grace," which outlines his pneumatology in light of his broader understanding of salvation.

Marshall, Molly T. *Joining the Dance: A Theology of the Spirit*. Valley Forge, Pa.: Judson, 2003.

Molly T. Marshall seeks to "find a way to speak of the pervasive presence of God as Spirit that reflects biblical patterns and historic spiritual wisdom and responds to new thinking about power and movement in our evolving world" (p. 11). Drawing on the theology of Jürgen Moltmann, she prioritizes the concepts of panentheism and perichoresis, and writes of the ways that the Spirit opens up space within the Trinity for all creation to participate in the dynamic life of God and be transformed. "We must speak . . . of the Spirit in connection with the body and nature, [and] with the evolutionary movement of creation and transformation through resurrection" (p. 14). Marshall emphasizes the empowering presence of God's Spirit, which she articulates not as a force that pushes or overtakes, but rather as an openness to the future. Her book is valuable because it creatively integrates recent trends in pneumatology that build on late modern scientific and philosophical shifts. More generally, it evidences the broad trend of connecting Spirit and spirituality, for Marshall explicitly aims not only to present a constructive pneumatology but also to invite her readers toward a deeper experience of the Spirit.

Maximus Confessor. *Selected Writings*. Translated by George C. Berthold. New York: Paulist, 1985.

Maximus was a seventh-century Eastern theologian whose writings were deeply informed by the works of the Cappadocian Fathers and Pseudo-Dionysius. For Maximus, it is by and through the grace of the Holy Spirit that humans are granted "fellowship and identity" with God "by participation in likeness . . . to become God" (p. 207). Consonant with key strands of the Greek tradition, Maximus drew a subtle distinction between the philosophical categories of *ousia* (essence) and *energeia/dynamis* (energies), and argued that humans are deified not through transformation into the divine substance but by participation in the divine energies.

McDonnell, Kilian. "Spirit and Experience in Bernard of Clairvaux." Theological Studies 58 (1997): 3-18.

In this article McDonnell, a Catholic charismatic theologian, sheds light on the important role experience plays in Bernard's theology, and in his pneumatology in particular. Focusing primarily on texts that treat experience and the Spirit together, he demonstrates ways in which "Bernard considers experience, delight, yearning as gifts from above, as allies of the intellect and will moving one to contemplation and union" (p. 17). Topics touched on include symbolism, the "stages" of experience, the ecclesial nature of the experience of the Spirit, the Spirit and Trinity, and the relationship between experience and faith.

―――. The Other Hand of God: The Holy Spirit as the Universal Touch and Goal. Collegeville, Minn.: Liturgical Press, 2003.

Written at the end of McDonnell's career, this book represents the culmination of his many years of work in the area of pneumatology. He interprets biblical and historical texts in light of his understanding of the Trinity and redemption as a "double movement" of all things from the Father, through the Son, and in the Spirit, back to the Father: "The Father sends the Son in the Spirit to touch and transform the world and church, leading them in the Spirit, through the Son/Christ to the Father" (p. 91). He speaks of the Spirit as "goal," demonstrating a concern for linking pneumatology with eschatology. He also insists on marrying christology and pneumatology; the Spirit is the "mediation of the mediator, Jesus Christ." Because he wants to emphasize the importance of beginning with experience in our attempts to formulate Spirit-doctrine, McDonnell also dwells intensely on various theologians' and mystics' unique experiences of the Spirit in prayer and/or contemplation. This book is a helpful overview of select biblical and historical theologies of the Spirit — especially patristic contributions — and is enriched with a constructive proposal that presents the Spirit as "the end point of God's journey to us . . . [and] the point of departure of our journey to God" (p. 115).

McFague, Sallie. Life Abundant: Rethinking Theology and Economy for a Planet in Peril. Minneapolis: Fortress Press, 2001.

Sallie McFague has entitled Chapter 11 of this book "Life in the Spirit." In it are only a few direct references to the Holy Spirit, but it speaks of the prophetic presence of the Spirit and its potential for transforming North American middle-class lifestyles of selfishness and greed. She seeks to inspire a new vision in her readers for the possibility of "the good life" construed not as a lifestyle of uncontrolled consumerism, but as a way of living that is reasonable in commodity and abundant in community, always oriented toward practical ways of empowering the poor and sustaining the planet. Clearly for McFague, an induction into "life in the Spirit" can be disruptive. "Minds, hearts, and wills must be changed in order for laws to be" (p. 199). McFague's chapter suggests that the Spirit of God is involved in the challenging of assumptions, the transforming of attitudes and actions, and the redeeming of the earth and its peoples.

McIntosh, Mark A. *Mystical Theology: The Integrity of Spirituality and Theology.* Oxford: Blackwell, 1998.

McIntosh's overarching goal is to recover and renew an appreciation for the mutually conditioning relationship between mystical thought and dogmatic theology. He contends that the divorce between spirituality and theology (and so pneumatology) that occurred in the early modern period has resulted in a lack of attention to the experience behind systematic formulations. He engages a wide array of classical and contemporary theologians, philosophers, and mystical figures, and articulates Christian theology and spirituality in a way that is expressly transformative, relational, and trinitarian: "Spirituality, in other words, is the activity of being led by the Spirit into Christ's relationship with the Father" (p. 152). Chapter 5 is especially noteworthy for our interest in pneumatology. There McIntosh presents a theology of the Holy Spirit as "God-in-the-other . . . the love which arouses us to full personhood by inciting in us a response to (and a participation in) the personhood of Jesus the Word incarnate" (p. 158).

McIntyre, John. *The Shape of Pneumatology: Studies in the Doctrine of the Holy Spirit.* Edinburgh: T&T Clark, 1997.

McIntyre's goal is to provide an account of major interpretations of the doctrine of the Holy Spirit, especially in the Reformed tradition. He offers an overview of major biblical texts that illuminate the identity and work of the Spirit of God, and extensive reflections on the ways the tradition has approached the question of the Spirit's role in the Trinity (particularly in John Calvin and Karl Barth). He also includes a discussion of "relational" pneumatologies, and addresses some of the ecclesiological dimensions of the doctrine of the Spirit. McIntyre acknowledges and affirms the diverse and manifold ways that the Spirit is experienced in Christian life, and interprets the Pentecostal movement with a hermeneutic of trust rather than suspicion. He also clearly prefers trinitarian models that emphasize the autonomy of the personality of the Holy Spirit, whose "external" work consists of "inspiriting," or "informing the spirit, heart, mind, and will of human beings" (208). At several points McIntyre locates the Spirit's specific personhood in *kenosis;* that is, the Spirit makes possible self-giving love in Christian life. Finally, he concludes by calling attention to three realms where the implications of the Spirit's presence in human affairs might be extended: nature/ecology, ecumenical dialogue, and the arts.

Milbank, John. "The Second Difference." In *The Word Made Strange: Theology, Language, Culture.* Oxford: Blackwell, 1997.

Milbank is a key figure in Radical Orthodoxy, an important development in contemporary theology. In this essay, his only piece devoted specifically to the topic of the Holy Spirit, Milbank seeks to articulate a rationale for a second distinction in God — that is, a pneumatological relation beyond the Father-Son relation. Rejecting "Catholic transcendentalist" and "Protestant Hegelian" solutions, he argues that the Holy Spirit must be understood within a linguistic, *Logos*-centered "aesthetics of reception." This leads him to suggest a distinction of the Spirit from the Son that is "grounded on the idea of a second positive difference which takes absence as the occasion for rhetorical community" (p. 189). In the economy of salvation, the Spirit is "incarnate" in the church and continues the atonement process by enabling humans to respond (testify) to the Word and become the image of Christ. In God's immanent life, the Spirit is positioned at a reflective distance from Father and Son as a listener, responder, and interpreter of the Father's spoken *Logos*.

Min, Anselm Kyongsuk. "Solidarity of Others in the Power of the Holy Spirit: Pneumatology in a Divided World." In *Advents of the Spirit: An Introduction to the Current Study of Pneumatology,* edited by Bradford E. Hinze and D. Lyle Dabney. Milwaukee: Marquette University Press, 2001.

Min's concern is to articulate pneumatology in a way that opens up dialogue in a pluralistic global society. Here he finds promising the idea that the being of the Holy Spirit "lies totally in being relational and creating relations," in other words the Spirit of fellowship and solidarity that can heal an increasingly fragmented world. The first part of his essay analyzes this cultural situation and the implications of the challenge of "solidarity of Others" for contemporary theology. The second and larger part outlines a doctrine of the Holy Spirit that begins with the idea of the Spirit as the "mutual love" of the Father and Son, but spells this out in terms of a view of the personhood of the Spirit that lies in the relating, reconciling, and creating of solidarity in both the immanent and economic Trinity. Min concludes by indicating hopeful signs of the movement of the Spirit and urging that pneumatology take concrete steps, such as moving beyond substantialism and toward a social metaphysics, becoming more politically conscious, and balancing flexibility and openness to the new with stability and appreciation for the institutional.

Moltmann, Jürgen. *The Trinity and the Kingdom.* Minneapolis: Fortress, 1993.

This book deals with pneumatology in the context of Moltmann's overall trinitarian understanding of God. Here he is particularly critical of modalist tendencies in Western theology, which he believes have had a deleterious effect on the doctrine of the Spirit.

———. *The Spirit of Life: A Universal Affirmation.* Translated by Margaret Kohl. Minneapolis: Fortress, 2001.

Pneumatology is woven throughout Moltmann's theology, but this book is his most comprehensive treatment of the doctrine of the Holy Spirit. Moltmann emphasizes (here and elsewhere) the immanent presence of the Spirit "in" the world and the existence of creaturely life "in" the Spirit.

Montague, George T. *The Holy Spirit: Growth of a Biblical Tradition.* New York: Paulist Press, 1976.

Montague offers a commentary on the principal texts on the Holy Spirit in the Old and New Testaments. As suggested by the subtitle, he finds a "development" in the tradition. He begins with the earliest tradition's emphasis on life-breath and prophetic impulse and the "charismatic spirit" of the Deuteronomist. He compares the pre-exilic prophets, with their emphasis on judgment and salvation, to the exilic and post-exilic prophets, who stressed the relation of the Spirit to the covenant. He shows how the priestly tradition pays special attention to the cosmic ordering role of the Spirit and its place in the songs and psalms of Israel. Montague also shows the influence of other ancient Near Eastern ideas of spirit and cosmology on the apocalyptic writings as well as the wisdom tradition and the community at Qumran. In his treatment of the New Testament he begins with Paul's early letters (e.g., Thessalonians, Philippians) and shows the development through his later writings and those usually attributed to his followers. Montague outlines the distinctive approaches to pneumatology of the four Gospel writers, as well as their similarities. He concludes with the use of the Spirit in other books, and finally treats what he calls the especially rich pneumatology of John.

———. "The Fire in the Word: The Holy Spirit in Scripture." In *Advents of the Spirit: An Introduction to the Current Study of Pneumatology,* edited by Bradford E. Hinze and D. Lyle Dabney. Milwaukee: Marquette University Press, 2001.

This article surveys the development of the understanding of the Holy Spirit in Scripture. Montague first covers key biblical images of the Spirit (life-breath, wind, fire, water, cloud, dove, paraclete). He then shows how in the Old Testament the source of the Spirit is God, and likewise, in the New Testament, Jesus Christ is shown to be "source with God." Finally, he summarizes the activity of the Holy Spirit in Christian life as seen in the New Testament. A unique aspect of Montague's treatment is that it highlights a gradual process of maturation in the biblical authors' understandings of the Spirit over time. This emphasis is in line with his earlier, more comprehensive work on the subject (see above).

Müntzer, Thomas. *The Collected Works of Thomas Müntzer.* Edited and translated by Peter Matheson. Edinburgh: T&T Clark, 1988.

This radical reformer is perhaps most well known for his violent resistance to the state and his criticism of Martin Luther, whom he argued was quenching the work of the Spirit in the church.

Oberdorfer, Bern. "The Holy Spirit — A Person? Reflection on the Spirit's Trinitarian Identity." In *The Work of the Spirit: Pneumatology and Pentecostalism,* edited by Michael Welker Grand Rapids: Eerdmans, 2006.

Oberdorfer highlights the significance of the fact that in the fourth century, when the theological meaning of the term "person" was being developed, it did not have the same meaning as the modern notion of individuality with self-consciousness. This essay provides an accessible overview of key moments in the shift in the meaning and use of the concept of person as it applies to the Holy Spirit. Oberdorfer also summarizes the proposals of Welker for the idea of the Spirit as a "public person" and Pannenberg's idea of the Spirit as a "field of power," arguing that these two emphases may complement each other so that language of the Spirit includes both the idea of a powerful presence and of intentionality.

Origen. *On First Principles.* Translated by F. Crombie. ANF, vol. 4. Peabody, Mass.: Hendrickson, 1994.

During the third century theologians focused more on debates over the concept of the divine *Logos* (or Mind) than on the divine *Pneuma*. Origen interpreted the Johannine claim that "God is Spirit" as referring to the divine Mind or intellectual nature.

Outler, Albert. "A Focus on the Holy Spirit: Spirit and Spirituality in John Wesley." *Quarterly Review* 8, no. 2 (1988): 3-18.

This article offers an introduction to Wesley's interpretation of his transforming experience of the Spirit.

Pannenberg, Wolfhart. *Systematic Theology.* 3 vols. Translated by G. W. Bromiley. Grand Rapids: Eerdmans, 1991-1997.

This is the magnum opus of one of the leading Lutheran theologians of the twentieth century. In Part I we point to the significance of his use of the concepts of "field of force" and "futurity" in pneumatology.

————. *Toward a Theology of Nature: Essays on Science and Faith.* Louisville: Westminster John Knox, 1993.

The last three essays in this book are particularly relevant for pneumatology. In "The Doctrine of the Spirit and the Task of a Theology of Nature," Pannenberg attempts to overcome what he sees as a typically Protestant conception of the Spirit as predominantly related to salvation rather than creation. Here and in the last two essays — "Spirit and Energy" and "Spirit and Mind" — he explores the biblical connection between Spirit and creation, critically appropriates theologians like Paul Tillich and Pierre Teilhard de Chardin, and suggests the general contours of an understanding of the Spirit that engages contemporary science.

Pinnock, Clark H. *Flame of Love: A Theology of the Holy Spirit.* Downers Grove, Ill.: InterVarsity Press, 1996.

This book by a leading evangelical theologian explores the classical Christian theological *loci* from an explicitly pneumatological viewpoint. In this sense, it is not only about the Holy Spirit, but an examination of the pneumatological dimensions of all aspects of Christian theology. For example, Pinnock argues for a form of Spirit-christology in which Christ is completely dependent on the Spirit. He suggests that the goal of salvation is to "live in loving union with God and to participate in the triune nature through the Spirit." For Pinnock, the Spirit is graciously present everywhere and in every person, leading the church along the path of mission. Throughout the process, he argues that the Spirit should be understood in terms of community (divine and human), which requires a relational ontology.

Prenter, Regin. *Spiritus Creator.* Translated by John M. Jensen. Philadelphia: Muhlenberg Press, 1953.

Prenter divides his treatment of Luther's pneumatology into two general parts: first, before the controversy with the enthusiasts, and second, the controversy itself (which he marks with the 1522 return from Wartburg to Wittenberg). He argues that Luther's later polemical efforts against the enthusiasts were not simply reactionary, but were an expression of a continuity in his pneumatology that takes the experience of an inner conflict as its point of departure for understanding the work of the Spirit (p. 209).

Prichard, Rebecca Button. *Sensing the Spirit: The Holy Spirit in Feminist Perspective.* St. Louis: Chalice Press, 1999.

Prichard uses the five embodied senses (sound, sight, taste, touch, and smell) as a hermeneutical scheme for organizing diverse pneumatological images found in the Bible and the Christian tradition. She calls for an interpretation of God the Spirit as "tangible" and "earthy," which she believes is closer to the biblical understanding than the "numinous, ghostly, and impersonal" interpretations that have often characterized Christian pneumatology.

Rahner, Karl. *Spirit in the World.* Translated by William Dych. New York: Herder and Herder, 1968.

Although this book is primarily a treatment of the human spirit, refiguring Thomas Aquinas's view of the intellect and emphasizing human openness to the world, it is important for understanding Rahner's broader concept of the God-world relation, and so bears upon his pneumatology.

———. "Experience of the Holy Spirit." In *Theological Investigations,* vol. 18. Translated by Edward Quinn. New York: Crossroad, 1983.

Rahner's goal in this essay is to explore the meaning and dynamics of the "experience of the Spirit" in human life. Although he does not dismiss "mystical" and/or "enthusiastic" phenomena out of hand, he prefers to emphasize ways in which we experience the Holy Spirit in ordinary, everyday life rather than in extraordinary moments of spiritual ecstasy. For Rahner, when we reflect on the conditions for the possibility of human knowledge and agency and are thereby awakened to the reality of an original, unthematic, pre-reflective experience of the "nameless unencompassable infinity" in and beyond the world, we are engaging in "transcendental" reflection, and we are also experiencing the Spirit. While this "transcendental experience of God in the Holy Spirit" is the implicit backdrop of each concrete, daily reality, Rahner argues that it is especially evident in those times and places wherein we surrender ourselves with unreserved hope and trust to the uncontrollable, incalculable, self-evident holy Mystery which transcends all things absolutely and is yet constitutive of our innermost being. "When, over and above all individual hopes, there is the one and entire hope that gently embraces all upsurges and also all downfalls in silent promise . . . when falling becomes standing firm . . . then we experience what we Christians describe as the Holy Spirit of God" (pp. 202-3).

————. *Foundations of the Christian Faith.* Translated William Dych. New York: Crossroad, 1978. Page references refer to the 2005 paperback edition.

Rahner was one of the leading Roman Catholic theologians of the twentieth century, and this book is his most comprehensive systematic presentation of Christian doctrine. He resisted Augustinian versions of the "psychological" trinitarian analogy between the human soul and God, and emphasized the divinizing presence of the Spirit who opens creatures up to the future.

Ratzinger, Joseph. "*Dominus Iesus:* On the Unicity and Salvific Universality of Jesus Christ and the Church." Vatican City: Congregation for the Doctrine of the Faith, 2000.

This is a significant document for ecumenical dialogue on the issue of the *filioque,* composed by the future Pope Benedict XVI. A full English translation of the declaration can be found in *Sic et Non: Encountering Dominus Iesus,* edited by Stephen J. Pope and Charles Hefling (Maryknoll, N.Y.: Orbis, 2002).

Reeves, Marjorie. *Joachim of Fiore and the Prophetic Future.* London: SPCK, 1976.

An introduction to the life, theology, and influence of Joachim of Fiore, who heralded the imminent arrival of the age of the Holy Spirit.

Reid, Duncan. *Energies of the Spirit: Trinitarian Models in Eastern Orthodox and Western Theology.* Atlanta: Scholars Press, 1997.

Reid offers a summary of the development of and debates over the concept of energies as it affected the East and West in pneumatology. Reid not only analyzes the rise of the issues that split the church over the *filioque,* but also shows how the two positions have shaped twentieth-century theology, and offers critical questions about how these positions in turn shape issues such as creation and grace.

Reynolds, Blair. *Toward a Process Pneumatology*. London: Associated University Press, 1990.

The explicit goal of this book is to take the first step toward articulating a doctrine of the Holy Spirit within the categories of process theology, which builds upon the philosophy of A. N. Whitehead. Reynolds argues that the Holy Spirit has specially to do with our experience of God as immanent in us and in the universe as a whole. After setting out an exposition of the idea of immanence in process theology, he treats the literature of Christian mysticism and ecstasy in some detail. He takes the latter to center upon the idea that one can appropriately envision oneself in an intimate, two-way relationship with God, and argues that Whitehead's philosophy, and especially his aesthetic (understanding of the feeling and prehension of all actual occasions) provides a coherent explanation of this reciprocity in a way that makes sense of religious experience, and in a way that classical theism fails to do. Reynolds concludes that the harmonious contrast of the subject's sense of conforming to the "divine aim" is what makes possible the breadth, depth, and intensity of feeling, which is the essence of beauty. "In this way Spirit experience is essentially personal transformation" (p. 182).

Richard of St. Victor. *The Twelve Patriarchs; The Mystical Ark; Book Three of the Trinity*. Translated by Grover A. Zinn. New York: Paulist, 1979.

The pneumatology of Richard of St. Victor (d. 1173) is shaped by his emphasis on the community of divine persons in the Trinity and his linking of the Spirit to charity and contemplation in spiritual practice. In *The Mystical Ark*, which is well-known for its creative, allegorical interpretation of Scripture, Richard points out that it is through the Spirit that the charity of God is diffused in our hearts. In *Book Three of the Trinity*, he argues that charity (love) is the pinnacle of all goodness, and describes the Trinity as the community of love in which the mutuality of charity between Father and Son overflows in the Holy Spirit.

Rogers, Eugene F. *After the Spirit: A Constructive Pneumatology from Resources Outside the Modern West*. Grand Rapids: Eerdmans, 2005.

Drawing from a variety of ancient and modern Eastern resources (including theological texts, liturgical texts, and art), Rogers outlines a pneumatology that depicts the Spirit as excessive Gift ("superfluity") in the Trinity and in creation. The Spirit "befriends" matter for the sake of the Incarnation, but this includes the whole of creation, over which the Spirit creatively hovers. This befriending takes concrete shape in the mortal embodiment of believers, in whom the Spirit dwells. Rogers explores four iconic New Testament scenes — resurrection, annunciation, baptism, and transfiguration — that reveal the Holy Spirit as the divine Person who gives and evokes abundant gratuity. "If she is super-fluous, her superfluity turns out to be the gratuity that gives grace and beauty in her interaction with the Son, who through her is allowed to receive what he already has so that others who do not have can share it" (p. 208). The Spirit is not simply opposed to matter but is the divine presence that transfigures matter, making it sacramental. He argues that this opens up new ways of thinking about "material" images of the Spirit in Scripture, such as water, oil, and fire. Rogers also suggests that our fear of connecting the Spirit too intimately to embodiment is a sign of a covert Nestorianism (the christological heresy that separates the divine from the human in Christ). He insists that the theological basis of such an intimacy is grounded in the distinctive role of the divine Spirit who rests on the body of the Son in the Incarnation.

Rosato, Philip. *The Spirit as Lord: The Pneumatology of Karl Barth.* Edinburgh: T&T Clark, 1981.

Rosato rehearses many of the criticisms of Barth's weak pneumatology, but he also believes that one may find resources in his theology for a pneumatocentric approach to theology. Part I of the book examines the ambiguity of pneumatology in Barth and points to intimations of the importance of the third creedal article in his early writings. Part II exposits the pneumatology of the *Church Dogmatics.* Part III is the most constructive, in which he suggests "improvisations on Barth's Spirit theology," playing out themes such as *Spiritus Creator* and proposing a revitalized Spirit-christology.

Sanders, Cheryl J. *Saints in Exile: The Holiness-Pentecostal Experience in African American Religion and Culture.* New York: Oxford University Press, 1996.

Sanders is a womanist theologian and ethicist. In this book she explores the history, beliefs, and practices of the "Sanctified church," that is, African Americans of the Holiness, Pentecostal, and apostolic traditions. The phrase "saints in exile" refers to the collective "dialectical identity" of the members of the Sanctified church who share a history of the Western chattel slave trade and the African Diaspora and who are heeding the biblical call to be "in the world, but not of it." The historical experiences of slavery and alienation from dominant culture by racial and socioeconomic injustices have resulted in the adoption of a new social ethic among Sanctified believers — an ethic that stresses personal morality, holiness in worship, and social justice. Sanders also posits that many of the elements of Sanctified worship (such as ecstatic speech, hand-clapping, and rhythmic dancing) have their origins in traditional West African religions and Diasporic worship rituals.

Schleiermacher, Friedrich. *The Christian Faith*. Edited and translated by H. R. MacKintosh and J. S. Stewart. Edinburgh: T&T Clark, 1989. Originally published 1831.

Considered the father of modern liberalism, Schleiermacher focused on the human experience of absolute dependence, which led him to be critical of many traditional formulations of the doctrine of the Spirit. He tended to speak of the Spirit primarily in relation to the enhancement of human reason and the unity of Christian fellowship.

Schmid, Heinrich. *The Doctrinal Theology of the Evangelical Lutheran Church*. Third edition. Revised and translated by C. A. Hay and H. E. Jacobs. Minneapolis: Augsburg, 1899.

This book is the most readily available English source for quotations on the Holy Spirit from the Lutheran scholastics from the late sixteenth to early eighteenth centuries.

Sheldrake, Philip. *Spirituality and Theology: Christian Living and the Doctrine of God*. Maryknoll, N.Y.: Orbis, 1998.

Sheldrake's book provides one of the best introductions to the historical problem of the divorce between theology and spirituality. He calls for an integration of the two, in which doing theology involves living out one's relation to God, and spirituality is the whole of life "viewed in terms of a conscious relationship with God, in Jesus Christ, through the indwelling of the Spirit and within the community of believers" (p. 35). Sheldrake also provides several case studies in church history that can provide resources for linking spirituality and the doctrine of God.

Shepherd of Hermas, The. Translated by F. Crombie. ANF, vol. 2. Peabody, Mass.: Hendrickson, 1994.

Written sometime in the middle of the second century A.D., this text illustrates a tendency among many Christian theologians during this era — namely, the lack of clear differentiation between the Holy Spirit and the Son of God (similitude V.6; pp. 35-36; IX.1; p. 43). *Commandment fifth* (II; p. 23) describes the Spirit's role in indwelling and sanctifying believers as they engage in a moral battle between good and evil forces within them. The divine Spirit is the bringer of visions, the inspirer of prophets, and the power that enables moral living.

Sherry, Patrick. *Spirit and Beauty*. Second edition. London: SCM, 2002.

This book is one of the few contemporary theological treatments of aesthetics that explicitly links it with pneumatology. Sherry claims that although Father,

Son, and Spirit are involved in every experience of beauty, the Holy Spirit, as the "point of contact with the Trinitarian life of God," is tied in a special way to aesthetic encounters. Drawing from a wide range of sources Sherry shows how the unique mission of the Spirit is to communicate God's beauty to the world. In natural beauty, human inspiration, and artistic beauty, the eschatological glory of the perfecting Spirit is revealed, giving us glimpses of the ultimate transfiguration of everything and the coming of God's kingdom.

Shults, F. LeRon. *Reforming Theological Anthropology.* Grand Rapids: Eerdmans, 2003.

Chapter 1 of this book outlines the philosophical turn to relationality, which is one of the major factors shaping the revival of interest in pneumatology in the twentieth century.

————. *Reforming the Doctrine of God.* Grand Rapids: Eerdmans, 2005.

The conceptual shifts outlined in this book bear directly on the task of "transforming pneumatology." Part I traces the challenges in the doctrine of God that became acute during the early modern period, viz., the notions of the divine as an immaterial substance, single subject, and first cause. The historical problems with these categories and developments in philosophy, science, and biblical scholarship that attempt to move beyond them are summarized. Part II outlines three trajectories in the late modern period that have responded to these challenges: the retrieval of divine infinity, the revival of trinitarian doctrine, and the renewal of eschatological ontology. Resources from the tradition with special reference to leading twentieth-century theologians are summarized, including the role of pneumatology. Part III offers a reconstructive proposal for speaking of God in light of these trajectories, in a way that incorporates language of the Spirit.

————, and Steven J. Sandage. *Transforming Spirituality: Integrating Theology and Psychology.* Grand Rapids: Baker Academic, 2006.

Chapter 2, "Reforming Pneumatology," provides an overview of shifts in late modern philosophy that play a role in shaping the conceptual space within which the doctrine of the Holy Spirit may be reconstructed today. In this context spiritual transformation is spelled out explicitly as the intensification of knowing, acting, and being in the Spirit.

Simons, Menno. *The Complete Writings of Menno Simons.* Translated by L. Verduin and edited by J. C. Wenger. Scottdale, Pa.: Herald Press, 1966.

Considered the father of the movement later called the Mennonites, Simons emphasized peaceful fellowship in the Spirit.

Smail, Thomas A. *The Giving Gift: The Holy Spirit in Person.* Lima, Ohio: Academic Renewal Press, 2002.

Smail provides an accessible and pastorally sensitive introduction to the Christian doctrine of the Spirit. As the title suggests, the "giving gift" is the overarching motif for interpreting the experience of the Spirit, and Smail uses this motif to explain the relation of the Spirit not only to the Father and the Son, but also to and in the church and world. Although he speaks of the Spirit as the divine "person without a face," this is only to underline the distinctiveness of the personhood of the Spirit, which he spells out not only in relation to the mutual self-giving of the Father and the Son but also with special attention to the dynamics of freedom, creativity, and glorification. For Smail, the self-giving love of God is opened up to creatures in the Holy Spirit. "The Gift who is the Spirit is God himself in gracious personal presence on our side of the relationship. He is the Giving Gift, because he enables us to share in the life and the love in which the Father, the Son and the Spirit have from all eternity had their being" (p. 214).

Smith, Steven G. "Topics in Philosophical Pneumatology: Inspiration, Wonder, Heart." In *Advents of the Spirit: An Introduction to the Current Study of Pneumatology,* edited by Bradford E. Hinze and D. Lyle Dabney. Milwaukee: Marquette University Press, 2001.

Smith differentiates between "general" and "special" pneumatologies, arguing that "philosophical" pneumatology can provide some warrant for choosing between or refining "religious" pneumatologies. Using the Christian idea of the Holy Spirit as his example, he also argues that religious pneumatologies cannot be simply deduced from or determined by philosophy, because the former have their own distinct resources and tasks. His analysis of the concept and experience of Spirit is spelled out with special attention to the ideas of inspiration, wonder, and heart. Inspiration, for example, is the idea of that which animates us and the world, and "wonder" has to do with the movement of inquiry in human persons and communities. He claims that analysis of inspiration cannot be indifferent to the way in which the Abrahamic vision of time is "a history within God's providence." In this essay Smith summarizes some of the points he had made in his earlier *The Concept of the Spiritual: An Essay in First Philosophy* (Philadelphia: Temple University Press, 1988), and applies them more directly to the Christian idea of the Holy Spirit. Chapter 1 of the latter book provides an introduction to the philosophical and historical background that shaped the concepts of the spiritual and the Spirit.

Sobrino, Jon. *Spirituality of Liberation: Toward Political Holiness.* Translated by Robert R. Barr. Maryknoll, N.Y.: Orbis, 1988.

Sobrino is a Latin American liberation theologian who argues that the spiritual life (which takes shape as active love for the poor) and academic theology (dogmatic interpretations of the experience of God) cannot be disunited: "I hold that spirituality is not merely a dimension of theology, it is an integral dimension of the whole of theology" (p. 49). For Sobrino, spirituality, theology, and acts of social justice are mutually conditioning. He emphasizes that the stirring, convicting Spirit of God is always compelling us to find innovative ways to actively work for social justice: "The Spirit of God continues to pronounce new words and make new demands. We can set no a priori limits to the will of the Spirit" (p. 5).

Stanton, Graham N. et al., eds. *The Holy Spirit and Christian Origins.* Grand Rapids: Eerdmans, 2004.

This is a collection of essays written in honor of New Testament scholar James D. G. Dunn. Each chapter deals with the Holy Spirit, making this book an excellent resource for understanding contemporary trends in biblical research on the key pneumatological texts of the New Testament, as well as the broader debates over the concept and theological appropriation of the term *pneuma.*

Staples, Rob L. "John Wesley's Doctrine of the Holy Spirit." *Wesleyan Theological Journal* 21, nos. 1-2 (Spring-Fall, 1986): 91-115.

Staples begins by showing that insofar as the Spirit was the mediator of Christian religious experience, and insofar as Wesley's approach to doctrine as a whole was not speculative but deeply experiential, it is natural to see pneumatology as central and regulative to all his teaching. He suggests that Wesley was closer to the Cappadocians than to Augustine although he did not deeply delve into those debates about the inner nature of God. The relation between Spirit and Word, which has been a debate among Protestants since the sixteenth century, is for Wesley inseparable, as for Luther, and Staples argues that Wesley's way of balancing them is key to understanding his theology. He then spells this out in terms of the Wesleyan emphasis on the "testimony of the Spirit" in relation to reading and interpreting Scripture, and on the "witness of the Spirit" in the experience of salvation.

Stephens, Bruce M. "Changing Conceptions of the Holy Spirit in American Protestant Theology from Jonathan Edwards to Charles G. Finney." *St. Luke's Journal of Theology* 33, no. 3 (1990): 209-223.

> Stephens offers in this article a brief historical overview of pneumatological developments during this important historical period in the United States.

Symeon the New Theologian. *The Discourses.* Translated by C. J. deCatanzaro. New York: Paulist, 1980.

> This text is a collection of thirty-four exhortations, probably delivered by this Spirit-centered mystic to his monks at St. Mamas. Seven of the exhortations are devoted specifically to the topic of the Holy Spirit.

Tabbernee, William. "'Will the Real Paraclete Please Speak Forth!': The Catholic-Montanist Conflict over Pneumatology." In *Advents of the Spirit: An Introduction to the Current Study of Pneumatology,* edited by Bradford E. Hinze and D. Lyle Dabney. Milwaukee: Marquette University Press, 2001.

> This article takes a fresh look at the historical background and theological issues surrounding the debates over Montanism, a late second-century movement that emphasized ecstatic experiences and prophetic utterances through the outpouring of the Holy Spirit, later condemned as heretical by the church. Tabbernee explores the key primary sources and attempts to show that the church came to view the movement and its leaders through inaccurate and negatively colored lenses. He concludes that many of the charges leveled against Montanism are "blatantly erroneous." He suggests that Montanism poses some enduring questions for the church, including those related to the validity of prophetic ecstasies, the extent of the fullness of the Holy Spirit's reception at Pentecost, the existence of progressive revelation, the nature of heresy, and what it means to live as a "spiritual person."

Taylor, Jeremy. *Jeremy Taylor: Selected Works.* Edited by Thomas K. Carroll. New York: Paulist, 1990.

> Anglican bishop and devotional writer Jeremy Taylor (1613-1667) struggled to integrate doctrine and spiritual practice during a time of great political and religious unrest in England. His rejection of the doctrine of original sin and his assertion that persons could really contribute toward their own spiritual progress through repentance and with the Spirit's sanctifying power led both Puritans and traditional Anglicans to suspect him of Pelagianism. Attention to the Spirit may be found throughout his works. Taylor views the Holy Spirit

as transforming everyday life and enabling persons to live in temperance, holiness, and moderation. "Wherever the Holy Spirit does dwell, there also peace and sanctity, meekness and charity, a mortified will, and an active dereliction of our desires, do inhabit" (p. 252). In his sacramental writings he highlights the empowering work of the Spirit, which facilitates dynamic spiritual growth through church ordinances: "The Spirit moved a little upon the waters of baptism, and gave us the principles of life, but in confirmation He makes us able to move ourselves. In the first He is the spirit of life, but in this He is the spirit of strength and motion" (pp. 255-56). Taylor believed that the Spirit's special dwelling in our hearts makes us "cabinets of the mysterious Trinity" (p. 447). He tended to shy away from rational or formulaic trinitarian proposals, instead preferring to emphasize experiential, spiritual knowledge of what he considered to be an ultimate divine mystery: "No man can be convinced well and wisely of the article of the holy, blessed, and undivided Trinity, but he that feels the mightiness of the Father begetting him to a new life, the wisdom of the Son building him up in a most holy faith, and the love of the Spirit of God making him to become like unto God" (p. 383).

Taylor, John V. *The Go-Between God: The Holy Spirit and the Christian Mission*. New York: Oxford University Press, 1972.

This book was written before the major revival of pneumatological reflection in the latter part of the twentieth century. Not only does it anticipate many of the theological themes that would become central in this surge of pneumatological interest, it also illustrates the dawning of an increased realization that lack of attention to the doctrine of the Holy Spirit has radical consequences for Christian life and mission. "If we had not relegated the Holy Spirit to the merest edges of our theology we might never have got ourselves into our present position" (p. 5). Taylor divides his book into two major parts, both of which are explicitly aimed at integrating pneumatology into the daily missional practice of the church. Part I, "Facts of Life," explores the dynamic role of the Spirit in the emergence of this life. The chapters in this section evoke the imagery of coming to life, including annunciation, conception, gestation, labor, birth, and breath. In all cases, Taylor emphasizes the power of the Spirit as the "chief actor" in the mission of the church. Part II, "Style of Life," examines the maturation and character of life in the Spirit. Here the chapters are organized around the themes of growing, exploring, meeting, playing, and loving. In this context, Taylor explores a variety of issues and practices at the intersection of mission and pneumatology, including interreligious dialogue and the growth of Pentecostalism.

Tertullian. *Against Praxeas, Treatise on the Soul, and On Modesty.* Translated by P. Holmes. ANF, vol. 3. Peabody, Mass.: Hendrickson, 1994.

Tertullian introduced the term *trinitas* and applied the word *persona* to the Father, Son, and Spirit. In addition to his trinitarian terminological innovation, he is also important as an early defender of Montanism, which emphasized the ecstatic experience of the Spirit. When Praxeas attacked Montanist forms of spirituality Tertullian accused him of serving the devil by chasing away the Paraclete in the Roman church.

Thomas Aquinas. *Summa Theologiae.* 61 vols. Blackfriars Edition. London: Eyre and Spottiswoode, 1963-1975. Paperback reissue, New York: Cambridge University Press, 2006.

Generally considered the most important and influential medieval scholastic theologian, Aquinas reinforced Augustine's approach to the Trinity and articulated the relation of the Holy Spirit to the creaturely experience of salvation in ways that engaged the prevailing Aristotelian philosophy of his era. In the *Summa,* his masterwork, Thomas treats the Holy Spirit most directly in questions 36-38 of the *Prima pars.* However, to get a full sense of his pneumatology one must be familiar with the whole of his trinitarian theology, which spans over questions 27-43 of the *Prima pars* (vols. 6 and 7 of the Blackfriars/Cambridge University Press set). Also important are his discussions on the gifts and fruits of the Holy Spirit, which are found in questions 68 and 70 of the *Prima secundae* (vol. 24 of the Blackfriars/Cambridge University Press set). Thomas also treats the Holy Spirit in many of his other works; see especially book 4, chapters 17-24 of *Summa Contra Gentiles* (Notre Dame, Ind.: University of Notre Dame Press, 1975).

Tillich, Paul. *Systematic Theology,* vol. 3. Chicago: University of Chicago Press, 1963.

This is a comprehensive presentation of Christian doctrine by one of the most influential Lutheran theologians of the twentieth century. Tillich focuses on the doctrine of the Holy Spirit in the fourth part of his Systematic Theology, which deals with the general relation between "life" and "spirit" and explores the specific Christian experience of "new being" in the Spirit. See Part I for a brief discussion of his approach to pneumatology.

Turretin, Francis. *Institutes of Elenctic Theology.* 3 vols. Translated by G. M. Giger and edited by J. T. Dennison Jr. Phillipsburg, N.J.: P&R Publishing, 1992. Originally published 1679-1685.

One of the most influential of the seventeenth-century Reformed Scholastics, Turretin's logical (elenctic) exposition of doctrine largely followed the Augustinian-Thomist understanding of the Holy Spirit. Turretin serves as a primary example of the Protestant Scholastic approach to pneumatology, which was later mediated to twentieth-century American theology through the efforts of Charles Hodge.

Van Dusen, Henry P. *Spirit, Son, and Father: Christian Faith in the Light of the Holy Spirit.* London: Adam & Charles Black, 1958.

Observing that "seldom if ever has an exposition of Christian Faith made its beginning with the Holy Spirit," Van Dusen undertakes precisely such an experiment in this book. After an introduction that provides a rationale for attending to the concept and experience of the Holy Spirit in the context of mid twentieth-century Western culture, he provides a summary of biblical depictions of the Spirit and a brief overview of the history of the development of the doctrine. The constructive part of the book explores particular theological themes "in light of" the Holy Spirit, spelling out ways in which beginning with pneumatology illuminates the Christian doctrines of man [*sic*], Christ, God, the church, and the Trinity. Although Van Dusen eventually collapses back into familiar modalist analogies for the Trinity, his book represents a significant early contribution to the twentieth-century revival of interest in the doctrine of the Holy Spirit.

Victorin-Vangerud, Nancy M. *The Raging Hearth: Spirit in the Household of God.* St. Louis: Chalice Press, 2000.

Victorin-Vangerud sets forth a "feminist maternal pneumatology of mutual recognition" that is situated primarily in "the groans and gasps, joys and anguish of postmodern feminist families struggling day-to-day beyond economies of unilateral power, coercion, and subordination" (p. 212).

Vischer, Lukas, ed. *Spirit of God, Spirit of Christ: Ecumenical Reflections on the Filioque Controversy.* London: SPCK, 1981.

This collection of essays is the fruit of consultations initiated by the Faith and Order Commission of the World Council of Churches in 1978 and 1979, in which prominent Eastern and Western theologians came together to discuss the historically divisive issue of the nature of the Spirit's eternal procession in the Trinity. The essays are organized into three sections; the first set treats historical aspects of the *filioque* controversy, the second set looks at then-recent developments in various traditions, and the third set outlines new proposals for agreement. Vischer's volume demonstrates the close connection between the ecumenical movement and the renewal of interest in the doctrine of the Holy Spirit in late twentieth-century Christian theology.

Wallace, Mark I. "The Green Face of God: Recovering the Spirit in an Ecocidal Era." In *Advents of the Spirit: An Introduction to the Current Study of Pneumatology,* edited by Bradford E. Hinze and D. Lyle Dabney. Milwaukee: Marquette University Press, 2001.

Wallace notes that the growing longing for the Spirit in culture is overshadowed by a pessimism about the prospects of our survival on earth. His thesis is that our best hope for renewal is founded on "belief in the Spirit as the divine force within the cosmos who continually works to sustain all forms of life." Wallace aims to move from a theocentric or anthropocentric to an explicitly biocentric model of the Spirit in nature. If the Spirit is thus connected to the earth then God is vulnerable to our wounding; Wallace accepts this conclusion and calls for a "green spirituality" that tends to the interconnections between all members of the biosphere. This essay provides an accessible summary of Wallace's main concerns relevant to pneumatology, which he spelled out in more detail in his *Fragments of the Spirit: Nature, Violence, and the Renewal of Creation* (New York: Continuum, 1996). The latter engages several postmodern philosophers, including Kierkegaard, Wittgenstein, Levinas, Girard, Ricoeur, and Derrida, applying their hermeneutical proposals to the issue of understanding and experiencing the Spirit in an age of ecological crisis.

Warfield, Benjamin B. "John Calvin the Theologian." In *Calvin and Augustine,* edited by Samuel G. Craig. Phillipsburg, N.J.: P&R Publishing, 1974.

Along with Charles Hodge, Warfield played an important role in mediating early modern Calvinist approaches to pneumatology to North American fundamentalism and evangelicalism.

Welker, Michael. *God the Spirit.* Translated by John F. Hoffmeyer. Minneapolis: Fortress, 1994.

A leading German theologian provides a careful analysis of the biblical material and philosophical issues relevant for pneumatology, and offers his own proposal for understanding the Spirit as a "public person."

————, ed. *The Work of the Spirit: Pneumatology and Pentecostalism.* Grand Rapids: Eerdmans, 2006.

In his own contribution to this volume, "The Spirit in Philosophical, Theological and Interdisciplinary Perspectives," Welker summarizes his critique and proposal from *God the Spirit,* and explores further possible directions for interdisciplinary development of the doctrine.

William of St. Thierry. *The Mirror of Faith.* Translated by Thomas X. Davis. Kalamazoo, Mich.: Cistercian Publications, 1979.

The writings of this twelfth-century Cistercian monk were rediscovered during the last half of the twentieth century. Like many other Western medieval mystics, he spoke of the Holy Spirit as the bond of love between Father and Son. However, he gave the Spirit a more prominent role than did many other theologians of that period. In this short treatise, William discusses the way in which the Spirit makes faith possible, and reveals truth directly to the Christian. He speaks movingly of the ways that we are "unexpectedly and entirely transformed" by the Holy Spirit. See especially Chapters 7 and 16, which are both devoted specifically to the experience of the Spirit.

World Council of Churches. *Signs of the Spirit: Official Report, Seventh Assembly.* Edited by Michael Kinnamon. Geneva: WCC Publications, 1991.

The WCC is a global ecumenical organization that includes member churches from virtually all Protestant and Orthodox Christian traditions.

Yong, Amos. *Beyond the Impasse: Toward a Pneumatological Theology of Religions.* Grand Rapids: Eerdmans, 2001.

In light of the Christian belief that the Holy Spirit is present in all of creation and human life, Pentecostal theologian Amos Yong argues that beginning with pneumatology opens up new possibilities for fruitful interreligious dialogue.

————. *Spirit-Word-Community: Theological Hermeneutics in Trinitarian Perspective.* Burlington, Vt.: Ashgate, 2002.

This book provides a detailed scholarly outline and defense of Yong's proposal for a "trialectic" hermeneutical approach in contemporary Christian theology that begins with the Spirit, but is integrally linked to the Word and the Community.

————. *The Spirit Poured Out on all Flesh: Pentecostalism and the Possibility of Global Theology.* Grand Rapids: Baker Academic, 2005.

In addition to its ecumenical and interreligious dimensions, this book also clarifies some of the debates within Pentecostalism over the relation of the Spirit to the other persons of the Trinity.

————. "Ruach, the Primordial Chaos, and the Breath of Life: Emergence Theory and the Creation Narratives in Pneumatological Perspective." In *The Work of the Spirit: Pneumatology and Pentecostalism,* edited by Michael Welker. Grand Rapids: Eerdmans, 2006.

Here Yong brings his work on pneumatological theology into dialogue with science. Taking Philip Clayton's theory of emergence as his primary dialogue partner, Yong explicitly argues against the assumption that the category of "spirit" must be metaphysically opposed to "matter." Rejecting the dualism of human body and human spirit, Yong suggests that a holistic understanding of personhood, such as that developed in Philip Clayton's theory of emergence, is more consistent with biblical pictures of human being. He observes that "biblical narrative acknowledges the dependence and interconnectedness between the human spirit and its material substrate in a way that is consistent with the emergent monist thesis" (p. 198). But Yong wants to expand this analysis in an explicitly pneumatological way, in other words, to explore the implications of non-dualistic metaphysics for our understanding of the relation of the divine Spirit to creation. He is critical of some aspects of Clayton's proposal, but believes that his metaphysics can be theologically bolstered by attending to the biblical emphasis on the Spirit's presence both over creation and in creation.

Zizioulas, John. *Being as Communion.* Crestwood, N.Y.: St. Vladimir's Seminary Press, 1985.

This Eastern Orthodox theologian has been one of the most widely engaged among Western theologians interested in trinitarian doctrine and pneumatology.

————. *Community and Otherness: Further Studies in Personhood and the Church.* Edited by Paul McPartlan. Edinburgh: T&T Clark, 2006.

Of particular relevance for the study of the Holy Spirit is the essay "Pneumatology and the Importance of the Person."

Index

Action: divine, 49, 86, 123; embodied, 77-78, 80-83; human, 7, 23, 130
Advocate, 2, 8, 31
Albrecht, Daniel, 70, 99
Ambrose, 99
Anderson, Allan, 68, 69-70, 99-100
Aquinas, Thomas 12, 41-46, 67, 102, 106, 136, 145-46
Aristotle, 12-14, 35, 38, 41, 50, 57-58
Arnett, William M., 62, 100
Ascetic, 21, 23, 24
Athanasius, 24, 25, 28, 29, 83, 100
Augustine of Hippo, 32-35, 100-101; as appropriated by: Anselm, 39; Aquinas, 42-44, 145; Bonaventure, 41; Burgess, 105; Catherine of Siena, 106; Coffey, 108; Dreyer, 112; Hodge, 66; Luther, 46; Rahner, 83; Wesley, 62. *See also Filioque*

Badcock, Gary D., 101
Balthasar, Hans Urs von, 88, 101, 120
Baptism: Spirit, 7, 8, 20, 38, 39, 48, 49, 69, 100, 121, 127, 128; water, 7, 8, 27, 29, 47, 48, 49, 90, 115, 138, 144
Barrois, George, 102
Barth, Karl, 82-83, 102, 138-39
Basil of Caesarea, 25, 26-27, 28-29, 102

Bergmann, Sigurd, 93, 102
Bernard of Clairvaux, 39-40, 103, 129
Boethius, 13-14, 85, 91
Boff, Leonardo, 80-81, 103
Bonaventure, 41, 103
Breck, John, 5, 103-4
Buckley, James J., 104
Bulgakov, Sergius, 83-84, 104
Burgess, Stanley M., 104-5

Calvin/Calvinist, 45, 49-50, 58, 59, 61, 62, 66, 74, 101, 106, 109, 114-15, 131, 148
Cappadocians, 24-29, 31, 32, 35, 62, 75, 102, 143
Catherine of Siena, 38, 106, 112
Cause/causality, Aristotelian, 14, 42, 52; and determinism, 34, 62, 92; in Eastern traditions, 26-27, 37, 74-75, 84; Final, 14, 42-43, 92, 58; and Trinity, 26, 32, 37, 67, 74-75; in Western traditions, 34, 42-43, 61, 52, 53, 59, 62, 67. *See also* Force
Chan, Simon, 106-7
Charismata. See Gifts (of the Spirit)
Charismatic: gifts of the Spirit, 18, 21, 23; expressions in early Christianity, 18, 21, 113, 114; movement in mainline churches, 73, 110, 126; and/or Pente-

costal, 68-72, 100, 105, 120, 121, 124;
spirituality, 99, 108. *See also* Ecumenism; Montanism; Pentecostalism

Clayton, Philip, 107, 149

Coakley, Sarah, 107-8, 121

Coffey, David, 86-87, 108-9, 112

Comblin, José, 80-81, 109

Come, Arnold B., 1, 109-10

Community: in feminist pneumatologies, 77, 78-79, 123, 130; in Hegel's pneumatology, 117; in liberation pneumatologies, 77, 81-82, 103; Moravian, 60-61, 126; New Testament and early Christianity, 6, 7, 8, 19, 114; Pentecostal, 69-70, 71-72, 149; in Schleiermacher's pneumatology, 64-65; spiritual transformation in, 19, 77, 85, 93, 123, 140; and Trinity, 79, 81, 103, 116, 131-32, 135, 138

Congar, Yves, 39, 53, 56, 73, 75, 107, 110, 116, 120

Constantinople, Council of, 24; Nicene-Constantinopolitan creed, 24, 75

Cooke, Bernard, 92-93, 110-11

Cosmos, 13, 14, 22, 41, 46, 71, 72, 80, 88, 92, 93, 102, 123, 147

Dabney, D. Lyle, 107, 108, 111, 112, 119, 120, 132, 133, 142, 143, 147

Davis, Stephen T., 73, 111

Deification, 25, 29, 37, 105, 116

Deity of the Spirit (defense of): in patristic theologies, 18, 25, 28, 29, 32, 99, 100, 115; in early modern theologies, 48, 60. *See also Pneumatomachoi*

Del Colle, Ralph, 112

Determinism, 14, 28, 34, 41, 49, 58, 88, 92, 95

Dreyer, Elizabeth A., 40, 112

Dunn, James D. G., 2, 112-13, 142

Eastern Orthodox traditions: as appropriated by: Bergmann, 93, 102; Burgess, 105; Congar, 73; D. Edwards, 87,

113; Reid, 137; Rogers, 138; and energies, 26, 35, 36, 37, 116; and Pentecostalism, 70, 71; relations with Western traditions, 30-31, 39, 43-44, 62, 70-76, 83-84, 91, 102, 108, 111, 147

Ecclesiology. *See* Community

Ecology, 64, 78, 90-91, 102, 124, 131, 147

Ecstasy, in early Christianity, 19, 20-21, 113, 114, 143-44, 145; in late modern pneumatologies, 84, 105, 108, 121, 126, 136, 137, 143-44; in Pentecostalism, 70, 121, 139. *See also* Charismatic

Ecumenical Councils: Constantinople, 24, 75; Ephesus, 30; Nicea, 24, 25, 100; Second Vatican, 55, 73, 115, 120, 124; Toledo, 30; Trent, 51-53, 55-56, 115

Ecumenism, 1, 10, 83, 104, 127; and *Filioque*, 31, 32, 37, 72-77, 87, 109, 136-37, 147, 149; and Pentecostalism, 70, 71, 120, 124-25, 127-28. *See also* World Council of Churches (WCC)

Edwards, Denis, 83, 87-88, 113

Edwards, Jonathan, 61-62, 113, 143

Einstein, Albert, 90

Embodiment, 23, 35, 48, 70, 91-92, 95, 138; in feminist and liberation pneumatologies, 77-78, 80-81, 90; spirituality/spiritual practices and, 48, 78, 104. *See also* ecology

Empowerment: in the biblical tradition and early Christianity, 3, 8, 9, 113, 114; experience of the Spirit and, 40, 48, 62, 69, 79, 110, 119, 124, 129, 144; of the oppressed, 78, 79, 80, 103, 115, 121, 130

Energies, 25, 35-37, 116, 137

Engberg-Pederson, Troels, 11, 113-14

Enthusiasts, 17, 45, 46-47, 48, 62, 71, 113, 135, 136

Eschatology, 46, 71, 76, 93, 95, 110, 112, 114, 123, 128, 130, 141; experience of the Spirit's eschatological presence, 46, 80, 83, 88, 95, 140

Eusebius, 21, 114

Fee, Gordon D., 2, 11, 114
Feminism, 77-80, 92, 115, 121, 123-24, 126-27, 135, 147; and liberation theology, 81, 86, 90, 91, 92; Spirit as "feminine" in God, 60, 79, 107
Filioque, 30-37, 39, 41, 43, 49, 58, 65, 67, 127; and Augustine, 32-35, 100; and biblical witness, 31-32, 86; and ecumenism, 72-77, 87, 108, 109, 126, 137, 147; and philosophical categories, 14, 32, 35, 37, 84, 91; as unimportant, 65, 127
Force: determinative vs. evocative, 28, 59, 85, 88, 92-94, 95, 129; human agency and, 14, 18, 59, 140; philosophical development of the concept, 12, 14, 32, 77, 89, 129; Spirit as "field of force," 85, 86, 91, 134. *See also* Cause/causality; Empowerment; Eschatology; Future
Fundamentalism, 62-63, 67-68, 72, 148
Future, creaturely experience of, 4, 5, 42, 80, 82, 92, 94, 95, 115, 123, 136, 137; of pneumatology, 89-95; as a theme in contemporary pneumatology, 83, 85, 87, 88, 92, 95, 129, 134. *See also* Cause/causality; Eschatology

Ganoczy, Alexandre, 52, 74, 114-15
Gebara, Ivone, 79, 115
Gift (Spirit as), 34-35, 36, 37, 39, 43, 46, 87, 100, 108, 110, 119, 138, 141
Gifts (of the Spirit), 6, 43, 45, 47, 73, 76, 102, 103, 145; charismatic/Pentecostal, 18, 21, 23, 69, 105; and institutional hierarchy, 21, 23-24, 81, 103, 114
Glossolalia, 68, 69
Gnosticism, 19-20, 23
God-consciousness, 64-65
Gregory of Nazianzus, 25, 28-29, 93, 102, 115
Gregory of Nyssa, 25, 27-28, 115-16
Gregory of Palamas, 36-37, 102, 116
Groppe, Elizabeth Teresa, 116-17

Guyon, Madame Jeanne-Marie, 117

Hebrew Bible, 2-6, 9, 10, 28
Hegel, G. W. F., 63, 64, 66, 86, 107, 117, 131
Hendry, George S., 1, 118
Heppe, Heinrich, 58, 118
Heron, Alasdair, 2, 5, 118-19
Hesychasm, 36-37
Hilberath, Bernd Jochen, 119
Hildegard of Bingen, 40, 112, 119
Hinze, Bradford E., 107, 108, 111, 112, 119, 120, 132, 133, 142, 143, 147
Hodge, Charles, 60, 62, 63, 66-67, 82, 120, 146, 148
Hollenweger, Walter J., 120-21
Hollingsworth, Andrea, 121
Humphrey, Edith M., 10, 121-22

Ignatius of Loyola, 51, 53-54, 55, 122
Infinite/Infinity, 12, 27, 44, 50, 61, 79, 87, 94, 95, 101, 107, 115, 136, 141
Interreligious dialogue, 1, 71, 83, 145, 149
Irenaeus of Lyons, 20, 26-27, 35, 81, 122

Jenson, Robert, 87, 122
Joachim of Fiore, 40-41, 137
John, the Baptist, 7, 112
John of the Cross, 51, 54-55, 123
John of Damascus, 29, 123
Johnson, Elizabeth A., 78-79, 123, 124
Justice, 4, 8, 40, 52, 80, 81, 86, 115, 124, 139, 142
Justification, 45, 46, 50, 52, 53, 58, 59, 67
Justin Martyr, 18-19, 124

Kant, Immanuel, 63, 64, 66, 107
Kärkkäinen, Veli-Matti, 70-71, 72, 124-25
Kendall, Daniel, 73, 111
Kim, Kirsteen, 125
Kinkel, Gary Steven, 60, 125-26
Küng, Hans, 73, 114, 126

LaCugna, Catherine M., 79, 126-27

Lampe, Geoffrey, 66, 112, 127
LaPlace, Pierre-Simon, 58
Liberalism, 62-66, 67, 68, 72, 139
Liberation, 77, 80-82, 85, 90, 91-92, 93, 103, 109, 115, 120, 121, 124, 125, 142
Logos, 19, 20, 23, 24, 87, 131, 132; as privileged over *pneuma*, 12, 18, 22, 42, 49, 108, 124, 134
Lossky, Vladimir, 37, 76-77, 84, 127
Love (Spirit as), 33-34, 43, 61, 100, 119
Luther/Lutheran, 45-49, 50, 52, 57, 58, 59, 60, 84, 87, 101, 122, 126, 127, 133, 134, 135, 139, 143, 146

Macchia, Frank, 71, 127-28
MacRobert, Iain, 70, 128
Maddox, Randy L., 62, 128-39
Marshall, Molly T., 129
Matter: and dualism, 19-20, 23, 42, 58, 78, 89-90; and immaterial substance, 32, 33, 36, 37, 63, 101, 140; and non-dualism, 90, 92, 93, 94, 104, 138, 149; philosophical development of the concept, 11, 12, 13, 14, 19, 20, 22, 58, 67. *See also* Embodiment
Maximus (the) Confessor, 35-36, 129
McDonnell, Kilian, 129-30
McFague, Sallie, 78, 130
McIntosh, Mark A., 10, 88, 130-31
McIntyre, John, 2, 131
Mechanism, 58, 84, 85, 92. *See also* Cause/causality
Medieval mystics, 35-37, 38-41, 53-55, 103, 106, 112, 119, 137-38, 143, 148
Milbank, John, 131-32
Min, Anselm Kyongsuk, 132
Moltmann, Jürgen, 85-86, 87, 92, 114, 126, 129, 132
Montague, George T., 2, 133
Montanism, 20-21, 23, 108, 114, 143-44, 145
Moravian. *See* Pietism
Movement. *See* Force
Müntzer, Thomas, 46-47, 48, 133

Neo-platonism, 11, 19, 38, 115
Newton, Isaac, 58
Nicea, Council of, 24, 25, 100

Oberdorfer, Bern, 134
O'Collins, Gerald, 71, 111
Oppression, 8, 77-82, 109
Origen, 22-23, 27, 234
Outler, Albert, 62, 134

Panentheism, 107, 118, 123, 129
Pannenberg, Wolfhart, 84, 85, 87, 92, 134
Pantheism, 63, 90, 94, 118
Parham, Charles F., 68, 128
Paul (the Apostle), 6-7, 11, 109, 113, 114, 133
Paraclete, 21, 22, 133, 143, 145
Pentecostalism, 68-72, 82, 86, 99, 100, 104-5, 113, 119, 120-21, 124-25, 127-28, 131, 139, 143-44, 149. *See also* Charismatic; Montanism
Perichoresis, 95, 105, 129
Perfection, 44, 65, 140; in Cappadocian pneumatology, 26-27, 28, 29, 88, 115; and final cause, 14, 42, 43; and Trinity, 59, 61, 81, 103
Person: Boethius's definition, 13, 14, 85, 91; experience of the Spirit's personal presence, 2, 7, 12, 28, 37, 46, 48, 80; of the Holy Spirit, 1, 12, 13, 20, 22, 26, 37, 41, 48, 62, 65, 74, 85, 86, 87, 118, 119, 122, 131, 132, 134, 138, 141, 148, 150; human, 3, 4, 9, 13, 23, 46, 52, 64, 78, 80, 81, 94, 95, 101, 116-17, 119, 120, 121, 123, 135, 137, 142, 144; philosophical development of the concept, 12, 13, 32, 37, 41, 74-75, 84, 85, 89, 91-92, 93, 119, 126, 127, 129, 134, 149, 150. *See also* Trinity
Pietism, 57, 60-61, 63, 125-26
Pinnock, Clark H., 68, 135
Plato/Platonic, 11, 12, 13, 14, 18, 19, 22, 23, 38, 50, 57, 58, 92, 115

Pneuma, 1, 12, 13, 14, 18, 42, 88, 104, 114, 121, 124, 134, 143

Pneumatomachoi, 25, 115. *See also* Cappadocians; Deity of the Spirit (defense of)

Pope Benedict XVI, 74, 120, 136

Power. *See* Force

Practices, spiritual, 23, 30, 31, 36, 45, 48, 49, 53, 54, 57, 60, 78, 93, 99, 104, 138, 139, 144, 145

Prenter, Regin, 45-46, 48, 135

Prichard, Rebecca Button, 78, 135

Process philosophy and theology, 88, 137

Prophecy, 3, 4, 5, 8, 18, 20-21, 70, 105, 114, 121

Protestant. *See* Reformation

Psychological analogy, 33, 37, 39, 41, 42, 59, 61, 65, 67, 83, 94, 100, 106, 136

Radical Orthodoxy, 131

Rahner, Karl, 83, 88, 92, 119, 120, 136

Ratzinger, Cardinal Joseph. *See* Pope Benedict XVI

Reeves, Marjorie, 41, 137

Reformation: Catholic, 51-56; Protestant magisterial, 12, 44, 45-51; Protestant radical, 12, 44, 45

Reformed theology, 49, 59, 61, 63, 74, 82, 85, 113, 131

Reid, Duncan, 35, 137

Reynolds, Blair, 88, 137

Richard of St. Victor, 38, 137-38

Rogers, Eugene F., 90, 138

Rosato, Philip, 82, 138

Ruach, 3-5, 9, 88, 103, 112, 118, 149

Sanctification: in early Christianity, 18, 23, 24, 30, 100, 140; in Catholic traditions, 52, 53; in Pentecostal traditions, 70, 121, 128, 139; in Protestant (non-Pentecostal) traditions, 45, 46, 50, 58, 59, 62, 67, 68, 100, 106, 119, 144. *See also* Deification; Salvation

Sanders, Cheryl J., 70, 80, 139

Salvation: in early modern pneumatologies, 45, 50, 52, 54, 58, 59, 65, 66, 67, 127, 129, 143; in late modern pneumatologies, 69, 83, 85, 92, 112, 121, 132, 134, 135; in New Testament and early Christian pneumatologies, 19, 20, 25, 26, 31, 32, 34, 35, 99, 103, 108, 114, 133. *See also* Deification; Sanctification

Schleiermacher, Friedrich, 62, 63, 64-66, 67, 82, 107, 112, 120, 139

Schmid, Heinrich, 58, 59, 139

Scholasticism, 10, 17, 38, 76, 77, 105, 112; medieval, 41-44, 145; Protestant, 57-60, 63, 67, 118, 120, 126, 139, 146

Science, 11, 41, 49; early modern, 12, 14, 44, 51, 57, 58; late modern, 71, 85, 89, 90, 91, 92, 93, 110, 129, 134, 135, 141, 149

Seymour, William J., 68, 128

Sheldrake, Philip, 10, 88, 139-40

Shepherd of Hermas, 18, 140

Sherry, Patrick, 88, 140

Shults, F. LeRon, 10, 11, 64, 94, 95, 140-41

Simons, Menno, 45, 48-49, 141

Smail, Thomas A., 74, 141

Smith, Steven G., 142

Sobrino, Jon, 80, 142

Sophia, 5, 79, 83, 123-24

Soul, 5, 13, 14, 21, 48, 84, 85, 119, 145; and faculty psychology, 33, 34, 42, 54, 100-101, 136; philosophical development of the concept, 13, 14, 19, 22, 33, 42, 54, 92; sanctification of individual, 58, 67, 68, 85, 91, 116-17; and spiritual transformation, 36, 41, 53, 54, 55, 56, 92, 103, 106, 123. *See also* Person; Psychological analogy

Spirituality, 19, 21, 23, 36, 47, 48, 102, 122, 134, 145, 147; charismatic/Pentecostal, 70, 99, 120, 121; liberation/feminist, 81, 121, 142; linking of pneumatology and, 9, 10, 62, 93-94,

106-7, 121-22, 125, 129, 130-31, 139-40,
141; mystical, 38, 112, 117
Spirit-christology, 86-87, 108, 112, 135,
139
Stanton, Graham N., 142-43
Staples, Rob L., 62, 143
Stephens, Bruce M., 143
Stoicism, 11, 12, 13, 14, 57, 58, 113-14
Substance: and deification, 25, 36; in
early Greek philosophy, 13, 35, 58; and
human personhood, 48, 54, 91; shift
away from the philosophical category
of, 49, 63, 64, 66, 79, 89-90, 92, 94,
107, 132, 140-41, 149; and Trinity, 22,
24, 25, 27, 28, 29, 32, 33, 34, 37, 41, 42,
43, 44, 55, 75, 83, 84, 100-101, 111. *See
also* Material
Symeon the New Theologian, 38-39, 143

Tabbernee, William, 21, 143-44
Taylor, Jeremy, 57, 144
Taylor, John V., 144-45
Tertullian, 21-22, 145
Theosis (divinization). *See* Deification
Thomas. *See* Aquinas, Thomas
Tillich, Paul, 66, 84, 112, 135, 154
Trent, Council of, 51, 52, 53, 55, 74, 115
Trinity: interpretations of, in Middle
Ages, 41-44, 145; interpretations of, in
New Testament and early Christianity, 6, 8, 19, 21, 22, 25-30, 32-35,
100-101, 105, 145; interpretations of, in
late modernity, 71-72, 79, 81, 82,
94-95, 103, 107, 110, 111, 112, 117-18, 119,
120, 122, 123-24, 124-25, 126-27, 129,
131, 132, 134, 136, 137, 138, 140, 141, 146,
147, 149, 150; interpretations of, in
Reformation and early modernity,
44, 45, 46, 48, 49, 50, 53, 59, 60, 61, 62,
63, 66, 67, 113, 115, 116, 126; Spirit as
"feminine" in, 60, 79, 107-8; spiritual
transformation and, 34, 36-41, 53, 88,
95, 101, 103, 106, 121, 130-31, 138, 144.
See also Filioque; Person; Psychological analogy; Spirit-christology; Substance; Will
Turretin, Francis, 59-60, 66, 82, 146

van der Maas, Eduard M., 69, 105-6
Van Dusen, Henry Pitney, 72, 146
Vatican, Second Council, 55, 73, 74, 115,
120, 124
Victorin-Vangerud, Nancy M., 79, 147
Vischer, Lukas, 73, 147
Voice, 4, 5, 6, 7, 8, 17, 40, 72, 77, 80, 111,
121
Voluntarism, 34, 95

Wallace, Mark I., 90, 147
Warfield, Benjamin B., 49, 148
Welker, Michael, 85, 86, 91, 111, 112, 125,
128, 134, 148, 149
Wesley, John, 61, 62, 100, 128, 134, 143
Will: human, 33, 34, 42, 45, 52, 54, 59,
60, 62, 91, 95, 100-101, 106, 127, 129,
130, 131, 144; Spirit as divine, 14, 34,
37, 41, 42, 44, 47, 54, 59, 60, 62, 67, 80,
88, 91, 95, 100-101, 106, 127, 142. *See
also* Psychological analogy; Trinity;
Voluntarism
William of Ockham, 44
William of St. Thierry, 148
Wisdom. *See Sophia*
Womanist Theology, 70, 77, 80, 139
World Council of Churches (WCC), 72,
125, 147, 148

Yeago, David S., 104
Yong, Amos, viii, 71-72, 124, 148-49

Zinzendorf, Count Ludwig von, 60,
125-26
Zizioulas, John, 74-76, 84, 92, 104, 150
Zwingli, Huldrych, 45, 47, 48